AF600384

NARRATIVE AND THE SELF

Studies in Continental Thought

John Sallis, general editor

NARRATIVE AND THE SELF

ANTHONY PAUL KERBY

INDIANA UNIVERSITY PRESS
Bloomington and Indianapolis

The paper used in this publication meets the minimum requirements of American National Standard for Information Sciences—Permanence of Paper for Printed Library Materials, ANSI Z39.48-1984.

Manufactured in the United States of America

Library of Congress Cataloging-in-Publication Data

Kerby, Anthony Paul, date.
Narrative and the self / Anthony Paul Kerby.
p. cm. — (Studies in continental thought)
Includes bibliographical references and index.
ISBN 0-253-33143-9 (alk. paper)
1. Discourse analysis, Narrative. 2. Self (Philosophy)
3. Languages—Philosophy. I. Title. II. Series.
P302.7.K47 1991
401'.41—dc20 90-28107

1 2 3 4 5 95 94 93 92 91

CONTENTS

ACKNOWLEDGMENTS

I would like to express my deepest thanks to Jakob Amstutz and Gary Madison for their generosity, friendship, and inspiration over the years. I am also indebted to Margaret Weiser for her careful reading of the manuscript at various stages.

Part of chapter 3 appeared in *Philosophy and Literature* (vol. 12, 1988) under the title "The Adequacy of Self-narration: A Hermeneutical Approach."

NARRATIVE
AND THE SELF

INTRODUCTION

> What visions in the dark of light! Who exclaims thus? Who asks who exclaims, What visions in the shadeless dark of light and shade! Yet another still? Devising it all for company.
>
> Samuel Beckett
> *Company*

This book is about the relation between language and persons. More particularly, it concerns that form of language called narrative and the various ways in which narratives and narration give meaning to what we usually call the self. Its guiding hypothesis is that the self is given content, is delineated and embodied, primarily in narrative constructions or stories. If we can substantiate this claim, then the self is perhaps best construed as a character not unlike those we encounter almost every day in novels, plays, and other story media. Such a self arises out of signifying practices rather than existing prior to them as an autonomous or Cartesian agent. This conclusion would, in turn, explain the difficulty we encounter when we attempt to discover the self by, say, some form of introspective vision, for there would, on this narrative position, be no "spirit" haunting this particular body that I claim ownership of. If we believe so strongly in such an internal subject it is perhaps because we have imagined such an entity to exist; we have either told, or somehow been misled by, stories and theories that posit such an ethereal being. This is not to say, however, that the concept of self is therefore unimportant and of no practical value, to be relegated to the ash heap of history. On the contrary, the development of selves (and thereby of persons) in our narratives is one of the most characteristically human acts, acts that justifiably remain of central importance to both our personal and our communal existence.

This book was initially inspired many years ago by a reading of works by Paul Ricoeur. It was conceived as an attempt to unearth the various roles that language and narration play in what we could broadly call "the life of the mind." This initial project is still maintained, but the focus is now on the self, that mysterious "entity" so central to the notion of mind. Accordingly, it is an investigation that will necessarily take us through a number of domains that traditionally belong to philosophy of mind (memory, imagination, and the like); but it will also venture into a number of related disciplines, such as literature, psychology, linguistics, and historiography. The reason for this diversity is precisely to give some indication of the interdisciplinary scope and importance of the investigation into narrative. But a further reason is simply that the recent philosophical interest in narrative receives its impetus primarily from a variety of sources outside philosophy. It is hoped, however, that the reader will discover in this diversity a sustained and coherent attempt to address many of the important questions that face us today concerning the nature of the self. The remainder of this introduction is intended to provide an overview of the general itinerary and a broad sketch of the main conclusions that will be worked out in greater detail in the chapters that follow.

An important factor that characterizes our present philosophical situation is its persistent concern with the nature and function of language. But this is no longer the old concern of how propositions relate or correspond to what has been called the "real world." This traditional epistemological concern, along with its metaphysical underpinnings, has been largely superseded by a deeper recognition of and investigation into the ways in which language plays an integral, even constitutive, part in almost all of our dealings with a world. From its primarily epistemological starting point, then, the investigation into language has received a relatively new ontological twist. Stated in its most basic form, language is viewed not simply as a tool for communicating or mirroring back what we otherwise discover in our reality but is itself an important formative part of that reality, part of its very texture.

Already in the romantic strains of nineteenth-century philosophy and in early investigations into the origin of language (especially Herder's), we see a rising interest in both language and expression as essential to the human subject. Later, with Nietzsche, language dramatically replaces this human subject with its own subtle web of metaphorical transformations. Simultaneously the systematization of hermeneutics by Wilhelm Dilthey places the question of language and textuality in the forefront of philosophical debate and enquiry. In our own century, Heidegger's rethinking of the hermeneutic enterprise, in *Being and Time* and in the later essays inspired by his readings of poetry, inextricably binds language to the world. "Language," says Heidegger in an often quoted phrase from the *Letter on Humanism,* "is the house of being." This remark is echoed more recently in the work of Heidegger's student Hans-Georg Gadamer: "Being that can be understood is language." These are perhaps enigmatic pronouncements, but they nevertheless attest to a shift of emphasis in some contemporary considerations of the nature of language. In contemporary Europe this initial shift is especially associated with the hermeneutics of both Gadamer and Paul Ricoeur, but the same story might also be told in the English-speaking world with the rise of conceptual analysis and the enormous influence on it of Frege, Wittgenstein, and speech act theory.

This story includes not only philosophers, however. Under the important influence of Ferdinand de Saussure linguistics claimed a similar stake in the rise to philosophical significance of language. This influence is felt all the way through structuralism into semiotics, psychoanalysis, the philosophical and deconstructive enterprise of Jacques Derrida, and important strains of contemporary literary theory. In their sometimes diverse ways all these views oppose the naiveté that considers language to be simply a more or less neutral medium of communication for ideas—indeed, for communicating facets of an external reality that does not require language to be what it is.

But what now of the subject who is, in some sense, the source of language? If on one hand language cannot be separated from the world as we know it, then on the other hand we surely cannot extricate ourselves from language. It is this other dimension, that of the human subject or language user, that particularly needs to be investigated today and that we shall pursue here, for why should we exempt ourselves from the very critique that we so readily apply to the world around us? We might now wonder: who or what is the speaking subject, the author of utterances? And what is meant or referred to by the little word *I* that proliferates in our discourse? These are the sorts of questions that must be asked, and asked from the linguistic paradigm in which we presently find ourselves.

The concern with language has, in recent years, begun to encompass what is undoubtedly a highly significant genre of language usage: *narration*. Studies ranging through sociology, psychology, philosophy, semiotics, literary theory, and historiography have taken up this interest in narrative, and it has become increasingly evident to numerous influential theorists and practitioners that narratives are a primary embodiment of our understanding of the world, of experience, and ultimately of ourselves. Narrative emplotment appears to yield a form of understanding of human experience, both individual and collective, that is not directly amenable to other forms of exposition or analysis. It is generally acknowledged, for example, that our understanding of other cultures and persons is primarily gained from, and in the form of, narratives and stories about and by those peoples.

The reason for this has to do with the way narratives articulate not just isolated acts but whole sequences of events or episodes, thereby placing particular events within a framing context or history. This form of contextualizing has, especially since Dilthey's hermeneutics and also gestalt theory, been recognized as crucial to any form of understanding. In hermeneutics this circular dialectic (which need not be construed as a vicious circle) is seen as one of parts and wholes: the parts can be understood only in relation to the whole they comprise, and vice versa. In light of this insight we are perhaps justified in concluding that it is especially through the unifying action of narration that temporal expanses are given *meaning*. In other words, isolated events need to be placed within a developing network of further acts if their broader significance is to be grasped. What I take to be the major revelation afforded by the investigation into narrative, then, is that it is precisely the privileged medium for understanding human experience, an experience that is paradigmatically a temporal and hence historical reality. Stated another way, it is in and through various forms of narrative emplotment that our lives—and thereby, as I hope to show, our very selves—attain meaning.

The guiding purpose of this book is to take the above narrative position seriously and draw out its consequences with regard to the nature and status of the human subject. What, for example, is the relation between language and the self, or between one's life story and the subject of that story? Such questions prompted me to develop a consistent view of self and self-identity from a primarily linguistic basis. Accordingly, what is offered here is a model of the human subject that takes acts of *self-narration* not only as descriptive of the self but, more importantly, as *fundamental to the emergence and reality of that subject.* This position will entail the related contention that "persons" are primarily the result of ascribing subject status or selfhood to those sites of narration and expression that we call human bodies. The person is thereby conceived of as an embodied subject. But this is not the embodied subject found in scholasticism or Cartesian modernism, a subject that retains in some way a metaphysical and problematic mind-body dichotomy. Perhaps we would do better to dispense with the concept of mind altogether; it is hoped that the present work opens up new avenues in this direction.[1]

On a narrative account, the self is to be construed not as a prelinguistic given that merely employs language, much as we might employ a tool, but rather as a product of language—what might be called the *implied subject* of self-referring utterances.[2] The self, or subject, then becomes a result of discursive praxis rather than either a substantial entity having ontological priority over praxis or a self with epistemological priority, an originator of meaning. Let me explain some of these points.

By *self* I mean the distinct individual that we usually take ourselves to be, an individual, therefore, that also knows itself to be.[3] Associated with this selfhood are modes of address such as *I, me, myself, we.* Selfhood also traditionally entails a degree of identity, of self-identity over time.[4] This self-identity involves believing or otherwise experiencing oneself to be, at least roughly, the same throughout a temporal span. I do not doubt that some such identity does or at least can exist.

One way to begin accounting for this identity is by positing some form of substantial self or agent that exists ontologically prior to the particular acts of the human subject (including linguistic acts). Such an underlying self can then serve as the basis or ground of an identity that persists throughout differing acts and other attributes; this is a fairly common belief. There are numerous sophisticated forms of this position, ranging from a religiously motivated soul substance to an idealistic transcendental subject. For many people, however, no real support is given for an underlying self other than the uncritical conviction people tend to harbor concerning their own abiding identity. Such views, if examined, tend to be metaphysical-theological or speculative in nature; they aim at explaining the identity that seems evidenced in our everyday experience by resorting to an underlying self-identical substance.

All such positions cannot be refuted, for their purely speculative nature may preclude this. But I do think that alternate and perhaps more fruitful descriptions (and explanations) of the self and of the person can be had, descriptions that put us on a somewhat different tack than looking for a specifically foundational and abiding subject.[5] The search for a foundational subject, as history teaches, tends to lead either to a mysticism wherein the existence of the self is assumed but cannot be demonstrated or to scepticism concerning the whole enterprise. I shall try to avoid both of these options and the foundational thought that gives rise to them. The position developed here aims at elucidating the constitutive role of language in self-formation and self-understanding, and seeks to answer all related questions from that basis.

In claiming that the self is a product, an implicate, of action, we are thereby removing epistemological priority from the human subject. That is, there simply is no self serving as the originator of meaning, something or someone to whom we might appeal in matters concerning the meaning or truth of his or her utterances as though these were prefigured in some nonlinguistic interiority of consciousness. Persons only "know" themselves after the fact of expression. This approach necessarily places considerable emphasis on both habit (as support for identity) and the relevance of context (for the meaning of acts), and goes against all forms of intuitive self-evidence or introspection that claims an epistemic transparency of the self to itself. The self is, we might say, decentered or displaced, removed from the epistemically central position given it by modern philosophy (particularly the philosophy deriving from Descartes). Correlative to this decentering is a loss of causal efficacy for the self and a stress on the subject's social setting, habitual structures, and, of course, language.

The subject's understanding of itself is, as contemporary hermeneutics teaches, mediated primarily through language, where language is taken to be the social medium par excellence. I shall therefore devote considerable space to the way the human subject finds expression for itself in its use of language. Of importance here is the way language prefigures a place for the subject in grammatical forms such as personal pronouns and adverbs of location (here, now, then, etc.). But what becomes especially significant within this linguistic view is the narrational nature of the subject's self-knowledge. The self, as implied subject, appears to be inseparable from the narrative or life story it constructs for itself or otherwise inherits. The important point is that it is from this story that a sense of self is generated.

At this juncture it is sufficient to consider narrative on the model of storytelling. Much of our self-narrating is equivalent to telling the story of our lives (or parts of it) from the perspective of a first-person narrator. Such narrating generally seeks closure (totality) by framing the story within a beginning, middle, end structure. Closure of this sort, I contend, is not only a literary device but is a fundamental way (perhaps *the* fundamental way) in which human events are understood. Failing this structure of closure, narrative at least aspires to followability, that is, to plotting a meaningful or "logical" development for our lives—which is not to say that it imposes linearity or simplicity on life.

Though I shall deal primarily with first-person narration, it should be clear that such narratives are considerably influenced by the social milieu in which the human subject functions. The stories we tell of ourselves are determined not only by how other people narrate us but also by our language and the genres of storytelling inherited from our traditions. Indeed, much of our self-narrating is a matter of becoming conscious of the narratives that we already live with and in—for example, our roles in the family and in the broader sociopolitical arena. It seems true to say that we have already been narrated from a third-person perspective prior to our even gaining the competence for self-narration. Such external narratives will understandably set up expectations and constraints on our personal self-descriptions, and they significantly contribute to the material from which our own narratives are derived.[6]

Self-understanding and self-identity will be dependent, in certain important respects, upon the *coherence* and *continuity* of one's personal narrative. Understanding, after all, is facilitated by a clear presentation and development of material, and identity implies a certain continuity over time. It should immediately be pointed out, however, that selfhood and identity, on our linguistic model, are not all-or-nothing matters. One's identity may be or become fragmented into many different and discontinuous narratives. That is, one may take oneself to be a different character at different times (as, in the extreme case, with multiple personality disorders), and this is perhaps more common than is often supposed. It should also be made clear here that my goal is principally descriptive and not prescriptive. I am not proposing that self-scrutiny and self-narration ought to be a primary and ongoing concern for human subjects; forgetfulness of self is also very valuable and in many cases necessary. I only hope to describe how the self in fact arises, in various degrees, out of our linguistic behavior.

For much of our lives a concern with self-identity may be marginal at best. Questions of identity and self-understanding arise primarily in crisis situations and at certain turning points in our routine behavior. Such events often call for self-appraisal. That we have, at any moment, the *belief* in a continuous and relatively unchanging identity is itself often little more than one story we have learned to tell ourselves—though it is, as we shall see, a very important story. Understanding the how and why of such narrational acts is a primary concern throughout this work. Let us now consider our narrative position in a little more detail.

Human existence is temporal—we grow older—but if we are to get at the more personal aspect of human existence we must see this temporality as a *history*. We indeed find ourselves, collectively and individually, embedded in an ongoing history.[7] When asked by others who we are, more often than not we are forced to give some account of our past life, and this will be predominantly narrative in form. Loss of this ability to narrate one's past is tantamount to a form of amnesia, with a resultant diminishing of one's sense of self.[8] Why should this be so? The answer, broadly stated, is that our history constitutes a drama in which we are a leading character, and the meaning of this role is to be found only through the recollective and imaginative configuring of that history in autobiographical acts. In other words, in narrating the past we understand ourselves to be the implied subject generated by the narrative.[9]

Self-narration is—and this needs stressing—an interpretive activity and not a simple mirroring of the past. In this respect, even fictions can provide us with characters and plots that we may identify with and which disclose ourselves; our experience of literature and film should readily prove this point. In the case of our personal narratives, "truth" becomes more a question of a certain adequacy to an implicit meaning of the past than of a historically correct representation or verisimilitude. I shall argue below (chapter 1) that the meaning of the past is not something fixed and final but is something continually refigured and updated in the present. This question of the truth of our narrations immediately involves us in the important and complex problem of the relation between the expressed and the preexpressed in human experience. Examination of this relation will be a pivotal concern throughout the later chapters.

This latter examination will involve showing that narrative is the form of expression most suited to portraying the vagaries of human experience. The basis for this belief is that our preexpressed, prethematic experience is already an implicit or quasi-narrative. Giving prethematic experience such a status implies the related claims that we always have a certain preunderstanding of our lives as being (1) historical, and (2) amenable to explicit (conscious) narrative exposition. In short, we know we are, in our lives, always already caught up in a story, already involved in a drama of some sort. This quasi-narrative background structure of our lives receives various degrees and varieties of articulation, though only with certain individuals (e.g., Marcel Proust) is there any pressing need or desire to express it in great detail.

This quasi-narrative position is not new. Stephen Crites, for example, developed such a position in an excellent article published in 1971. He attributes to human experience a "narrative quality" that may be viewed as an "incipient story." He adds: "In principle, we can distinguish between the inner drama of experience and the stories through which it achieves coherence. But in any actual case the two so interpenetrate that they form a virtual identity. . . ."[10] This storied nature of our experience is, for Crites, what holds the past (memory) and future (anticipation) together in the present, creating the more or less unified sense we have of our ongoing lives, a sense upon which our personal identity so thoroughly depends.

In this book, then, the term *quasi-narrative* refers to the general structure of our experience or, in other words, of our ongoing lives. Quasi-narrative is to be distinguished from the consciously worked-up narratives that we find in historical and biographical works and from the narratives that we explicitly or consciously give of ourselves and others. There is, however, an intimate connection between these two forms of narrative, as we shall see below. Explicating and developing this connection is in fact one of the central concerns throughout this work.

With respect to self-understanding, the quasi-narrative nature of our experience accounts for the ongoing sense of orientation and purpose our lives generally exhibit. It is out of this narrative preunderstanding that the explicit self-narrations of our lives are formed—though not in a strictly one-to-one relation. We might say, in Kantian fashion, that the quasi-narrative nature of experience is the condition of possibility for the stories we tell of ourselves, but we must add that explicit narration may take up and reconfigure this implicit narrative structure in various ways (selecting, augmenting, and such like); this is usually what is happening when we recount, say, past episodes of our lives.

I will often refer to this quasi-narrative structure as the *prenarrative level* of experience, where the prefix should be taken to imply not the complete absence of narrative, as though it were prior to all narrative structure, but rather an earlier (and in a sense more primitive) stage of narrative structuration. This latter distinction should become clear as we proceed.

Although we are not self-consciously narrating ourselves all the time, narrational activity of some sort is common to a great deal of our experience—from dreams to memory to future plans from emotional to moral experience. We may also have a sense of participating in many stories at once, even though these stories are not explicitly narrated or focused upon. Such stories may also be at odds with one another (a conflict that could, for example, easily cause emotional disturbances), or they may be circumscribed and perhaps justified by yet another all-encompassing story. Both self-understanding and self-identity are linked with the coherence of our lives as reflected in our personal narratives. However, the nature of the prenarrative level of experience will usually preclude just any story being constructed; there is an interesting dialectical relation to be uncovered here.[11] Accordingly, I hope to show that self-narration is both a receptive and a creative activity, receptive in relation to embodying or expressing our prenarrative experience and creative in the way our conscious narratives inevitably refigure and augment the prenarrative level of experience.

Before offering the reader a brief overview and guide to the main chapters, I would like to sketch out the general intellectual arena within which this enterprise fits and from which it draws much of its substance and inspiration.

Vincent Descombes recently traced the development of French philosophy since Bergson through three important stages, which in turn represent three "advances" in our conceiving of the epistemic relation of the knowing subject to the "external world."[12] The first stage is the "phenomenological victory over the 'philosophy of representation,' thanks to the concept of intentionality." This stage was prefigured in Husserl's exhortation *zu den Sachen selbst,* which carries over into Sartrean philosophy and phenomenological existentialism generally. Important to the phenomenological perspective is the unmediated presence of the human subject to the world and its phenomenal contents, which in turn entails a rejection of the Kantian *Ding an sich* and the metaphysical tradition that prefigures it. The second stage isolated by Descombes is the "hermeneutic victory over 'onto-theology,' thanks to the concept of interpretation." From Nietzsche and Dilthey up to Heidegger, Gadamer, Jürgen Habermas, and Ricoeur, this philosophical stance stresses human finitude and the partiality of our knowledge of the world. The last of Descombes's stages is the "semiological victory over the 'metaphysics of the referent,' thanks to the revolutionary new concept of the sign." This semiological position, though evident in both Peirce and, to some degree, Wittgenstein, derives its contemporary impetus (which extends to a number of humanistic disciplines) especially from Saussurian linguistics and has motivated French thought up to its present deconstructive and postmodern representatives. Says Descombes:

> The discovery of the true nature of the sign is the thesis whereby a sign derives its meaning not from its relation to an independent thing . . . but from its relation to other signs inside a closed system.[13]

These three philosophical positions show an interesting and not arbitrary historical development.[14] All three can be viewed as a reaction against a metaphysics that seeks being *(ousia, Sein)* beyond experience, that is, in a metaphysical referent beyond the given. Phenomenology especially emphasizes what Merleau-Ponty called the "primacy of perception" (that, to put it crudely, to be is to be perceived from the perspective of a human subject), while the second, hermeneutics, stresses that our knowledge of such being cannot escape from the historicity and locatedness of our gaze. There is thus no pure insight into being—an insight that could grasp the presupposed untainted intelligibility of things. The third position, semiotics, shifts this whole epistemological-metaphysical debate onto another level by firmly rejecting extralinguistic reference as being "the unilateral measure of the validity of our assertions," to quote Descombes. The acquisition of knowledge would then be, to borrow from Wittgenstein, the learning and extension of new language games. This latter position, which Descombes identifies with semiotics, could however lead to an outright linguistic relativism or mere word play if it were not tempered by the life practices it both serves and gives rise to. The notion of reference should not, I suggest, be entirely abandoned, but should be recognized precisely as problematic, perhaps as one of the few central problems characterizing contemporary thought. Such caution will serve to exclude both its naive rehabilitation and its outright rejection.

It is my belief that these three positions, as outlined, are all of value, that their central insights should be integrated, and that contemporary hermeneutics can best be viewed as usefully fulfilling this task; the work of Ricoeur can be seen as one example of such attempted integration. On one hand, a hermeneutic philosophy can accept the phenomenological starting point of the human subject's immediacy to phenomena. However, it does not delude itself into thinking that there is a privileged mode of access to phenomena that would disconnect the categories of our particular historical and linguistic heritage. On the other hand, while recognizing that our understanding is mediated by language and semiotic systems generally—the signifying networks of exchange and communication between human subjects—hermeneutics need not lose contact with the life experiences of the subjects within this broad semiotic realm. That is, we not only come to understand the sign systems operative in our world, but also, to some degree, ourselves as we live and interact in and through them. As Ricoeur has constantly stressed, semiotics (and structuralism) has still to take the final step of accounting for the experiencing subjects presupposed by any structural social system.[15] Semiotics would, at its extreme point, remain arbitrary with respect to phenomenal experience, just as phenomenology would remain silent if it were consistently to avoid the conceptual and cultural biases of our languages.

This methodological interlude is intended to set the scene for all that follows. Hermeneutics in the form just outlined will be a guiding, though often implicit, philosophical stance throughout, but this will not prevent our accepting many important insights from both the phenomenological and the semiotic traditions (including their deconstructive and poststructural inheritors).

There are two further and important methodological points to keep in mind here. First, I shall restrict my philosophical exposition to describing human experience from the point of view of language-using human subjects *already* enmeshed in social reality (the *Lebenswelt*). This philosophical stance will preclude my venturing into metaphysical speculation on the origins of, say, language or consciousness. Similarly, my phenomenological commitment avoids consideration of the human subject from a traditional empirical or naturalistic standpoint. For example, whether or not events of meaning, significance, understanding, and the like can be reduced to functionings on the physical-chemical level of scientific inquiry will not be of concern to us here, for such models and hypotheses rarely if ever connect with the *experience* human subjects have of themselves as meaningful, understanding, self-reflective social subjects.[16]

Second, though the semiotic realm (language, advertising, animal gestures, art, and so on) is far broader than what we ordinarily mean by the term *language*,[17] I shall nevertheless restrict the discussion principally to language (spoken and written). Many other semiotic fields in the human sphere both presuppose and utilize ordinary language, and this to the degree that one is justified in calling such language the preeminent or privileged sign system of human intercourse. Neither visual art nor music, for example, serves as the social medium in which our everyday interpersonal transactions are carried out. It is closer to the truth to say that we exist as a speech community within which such semiotic systems and symbolic activities arise as vocational activities. That it might be possible to gain some form of self-understanding and sense of personal identity to the exclusion of linguistic competence is, I believe, secondary to a consideration of the human subject qua language user and will not, therefore, be a primary question in this work. I hope that my conclusions will be seen to support this claim. I begin with what has been called the "language animal," with the aim of describing the nature of self and self-identity that this dominant characteristic of our lives entails.[18]

In brief, what is attempted in this book is to draw out and integrate insights from the works of important contemporary thinkers (primarily from all three of the above "traditions") that are relevant to the central theme of self and personhood. The investigation should yield what I take to be a properly hermeneutic, indeed postmodern, view of the human subject—that is, a view that places particular importance on the role of both language and interpretation to the very constitution of what we generally mean by a self-conscious human subject.

Rather than begin in medias res with the narrative subject, we shall work our way toward this position through an initial consideration of time and memory (chapter 1). The section headed "The Time of Our Lives" brings into focus the historicality and connectedness of human experience, the temporal structure of our lives as a cumulative process of sedimented meanings. This sedimented history serves as the horizon within which our present acts take on meaning. Self-understanding will involve thematizing our history in recollective acts. Accordingly, the next section is an examination of memory and recollection. It is with recollection that the past is actively appropriated to the self. But this appropriation, as we shall see, is always an interpretation of the past, a selective and imaginative retelling of it from the perspective of the present. This first chapter will prepare us for the explicit consideration of the narrative nature of our experience and of our self-knowledge. I shall argue that if experienced time is basically the time of our lives—our history—it is through narrative that this history is recounted. The consideration of memory will lead us to this conclusion.

Chapter 2 deals explicitly with narrative and its relation to the self and self-identity. At this point, however, and in line with the previous chapter, the discussion will be limited to narrative as it figures in the makeup of our daily lives. An important goal of this and later chapters is to show that narrative structures are indigenous to human experience and are not simply an imposition of art on life: the art-to-life relation is a two-way street.

The first section, "I Am I," aims at discrediting the view that the self is immediately given to itself through some introspective intuition. I shall argue, following Alasdair MacIntyre and Hannah Arendt, that one's identity is that of a character in a narrative and that self-understanding is accordingly a matter of the emplotment of one's experiences. These latter themes are taken up in more detail in the second section, "The Story of Our Lives," which develops the theme of narrative as a mode of understanding. The primary problem tackled here is the relation between the narrative and prenarrative levels of experience. I shall argue, against Louis Mink and invoking Ricoeur, that narration of oneself is both a receptive and a creative activity, that the implicit narrative structure of life is taken up and augmented in our explicit narratives. The goal is to show that we are always already caught up in narratives and that we are primarily, as MacIntyre has said, storytelling animals.

The remaining sections attempt to back up these claims concerning the thoroughgoing importance of narrative in our lives by considering its importance to both our emotional experience and to morality. The third section, "Narrative and Emotion," examines the work of Charles Taylor on the importance of language and interpretation for our emotional experience. The claim here is that the higher or, as Taylor calls them, subject-referring emotions are inseparable from an autobiographical articulation that itself discloses value directions in the person's life. Emotions, it will be argued, both call forth narrative articulation and are themselves based on some degree of narrative understanding of events. The fourth section, "The Virtue of Narrative," considers the way in which the value of an event is dependent upon how we narrate that event. The primary claim here is that narration rarely if ever escapes being evaluative. As social beings we are already indoctrinated into certain traditional narratives that set up "standard" expectations and obligations and that guide our explicit evaluations; narrative, as Jean-François Lyotard has claimed, is a primary vehicle of ideology.

In chapter 3 we move away from a general discussion of narrative to a more particular consideration of the individual in relation to language. I shall pursue, in greater detail than before, both the nature of spoken language and the development of self-consciousness with language usage. The first section, "He Who Says 'Ego'" studies the formation of selfhood and self-consciousness as these arise through the use of the first-person singular and recognition of its dialectical relation to the second person. The analysis proceeds via consideration of the linguist Emile Benveniste's important writings on language and the human subject. The second section, "Signs of Derrida," complements the earlier discussion of narrative by considering the soliloquizing subject and arguing against the position of language as, in essence, a means of communicating prefigured intentions. I shall argue, with Derrida and against Husserl, that meaning arises from and requires the presence of signifiers and their iterability. The third section, "The Alter Ego," examines the way language usage introduces a split in the subject between what I shall call the *speaking* and the *spoken* subjects. Of importance here will be a discussion of Jacques Lacan's mirror stage of ego development. The fourth section, "Narrative and Truth," draws some important conclusions, on the basis of the above sections, concerning the problematic relation of self-narration and truth. I shall argue for a pragmatic rather than a representational theory of truth in this area. The discussion concludes with a consideration of the similarity of the problems of self-narration and the writing of history.

After a last criticism of the Cartesian cogito, the final section, "The Semiotic Subject," draws together our previous investigations into the self and self-narration by arriving at a systematization of the human subject into three primary moments: the speaking subject, the subject of speech, and the spoken subject. Briefly, these three subjects represent the three aspects of human expression. The speaking subject is the individual qua site of expression—the language user. The subject of speech is the purely signified subject of utterances, that is, the subject qua position within a signifying network without consideration of the flesh-and-blood author of the utterance; in other words, the subject projected by, or meant in, the utterance. Finally, the spoken subject is the audience of the utterance or the subject qua listener or receiver, the individual affected by the utterance. A rough but perhaps useful parallel can be drawn between the three subjects outlined above and the more often encountered division, from the literary sphere, between narrator, character, and spectator.

A cautionary note. General language usage predisposes us to conceive of the self in a way that is usually at odds with what I am proposing here. As

Nietzsche has said, language leads us to posit a substantial "doer before the deed." In light of such common expressions as "I think," "I walk," "I remember," there is a strong tendency to believe in a self existing outside those acts, a self that is their motivator. Although I shall argue against this motivator position—this will indeed be a major focus in what follows—it is nevertheless very difficult to avoid the structure of language that supports it. While I find it acceptable and perhaps unavoidable to say "I think," I would not want to suggest by this usage that there is a prelinguistic entity (some inner I) that does the thinking. Using *I*, as in the beginning of the last sentence, is not only difficult to avoid but of course becomes doubly problematic in a treatise that seeks gradually to unfold a possible meaning for the I and the self. I must trust that the reader will bear this precaution in mind, especially in the early chapters.

A concluding note. From a hermeneutic perspective there can be no such thing as a final "truth" of the human subject and the human condition, for we investigators are not the disengaged spectators that such a scientific inquiry would require. We are ourselves the subject of the inquiry, and the asking of the question regarding the nature of the human subject is a considerable part of what it means to be such a subject. Thus I cannot claim the venerable status of the "truth" for what is contained in these pages. What is hoped for is that the reader finds this interpretation of the human subject to be both a plausible and a coherent account, and at times perhaps even a provocative one.[19]

I

TIME AND MEMORY

> We are, as Proust declared, perched on a pyramid of past life, and if we do not see this, it is because we are obsessed by objective thought.
>
> Maurice Merleau-Ponty
> *Phenomenology of Perception*

The Time of Our Lives

If we wish to grasp the nature of our specifically human existence, an existence that has a certain self-identity and consciousness of that identity, it is appropriate to begin our investigation with the question of temporally, for if one thing is to be admitted, it is that our lives are temporally determined both by the beginning and the end that our physical being exhibits and by the history that threads between, and even beyond these two poles. I do not think that what we call our self or our identity can be adequately considered outside this temporal and therefore historical framework, outside the time of our lives. When we ask of someone *who* they are, this question generally comes down to a recounting of their passage through time, their autobiography or self-narrative. Already we are talking not merely of temporality as a cosmic phenomenon, of the mere movement of bodies, for example, but of a time whose events are precisely the events in a person's life. This latter form of temporality is always *someone's*.

We could say, with Heidegger, that *Dasein* (human being) is temporalizing in its very essence. This claim leads one to the position that time is not simply something objective, belonging to what we often call nature, but in addition, and even prior to this, characterizes any being that can set up such an objective realm for itself. Human existence seems in all respects temporal. Accordingly, what must not be lost sight of during the following analysis is that the temporality we seek to describe is that which is most intimate to the human subject, that which is often overlooked due to its very proximity.

This is not to say, however, that temporality is the necessary form of intuitive apprehension for an "I" that itself escapes this temporal constraint, as it was for the Kantian transcendental philosophy. The "I" is caught up in this temporalizing, is itself inseparable from it, and we shall later have occasion to consider the substantiating of this "I." Initially, and in accord with general phenomenological and therefore descriptive principles, we shall hold firm to experience itself as the horizon within which all objectivities make their appearance, and we will at first presuppose as little as possible concerning the being to whom they appear. This latter being is precisely the problem under investigation in these chapters. A further point: at this early stage we shall remain primarily on the precognitive or passive level of experience. How this level gives rise to or otherwise connects with explicit self-consciousness will be the task of later chapters.

Experience is *at once* part and whole. The concept of experience can be used to cover the whole of a life ("There is nothing but experience"), and also the parts of a life ("I just had a strange experience"). Another way of saying this is that experiences come to one not in discrete instances but as part of an ongoing life, *my* life. Experience gains its density and elusiveness precisely through a continuous contextualizing or meshing of part to changing whole; the relating of itself to itself. In a similar vein Merleau-Ponty, in the *Phenomenology of Perception,* particularly stressed that "now" is not atomistic but variable, depending on one's perspective, one's interest. "Now" can be "this moment," "this day," "this year," or "this life." It is as though experience is disclosed in the manner of a set of Chinese boxes, one fitting perfectly inside or around another. Experience is in this sense overdetermined; it has an ever unfolding richness or expanse before our reflective gaze. And what applies to experience can also be said, as our example of nowness illustrates, for time.

We wish to consider time as a primary modality of this life that we are. However, much of the philosophical controversy over the nature of our identity arises from the tendency of analyzing experience in terms of component parts only, and of attempting to reconstruct the unity of our lived experience therefrom. One presupposes that experience, in accordance with an objective and reductionist view of time, comes initially in units and that one's philosophical task is to propose how these units become linked into a unitary chain. But this is to bias philosophical inquiry from the beginning rather than to attempt a more unbiased description of our experience. Perhaps all such problems of unification relate to the age-old metaphysical question of identity and difference, or the one and the many.

While reducing experience to component parts we nevertheless tend also to harbor a firm belief in the unity and coherence of our life, for we generally believe in our identity over time. Identity and difference are here set up as two unfriendly poles of the same concern; we simply attempt the resolution from A to Z or from Z to A. Perhaps, however, the identity and difference scheme only applies to life in the same manner as Merleau-

Ponty's "now," which is, and without contradiction, both this day and this year, both one day and many. The experience of our identity is in fact so interwoven with difference that neither pure identity nor pure difference can be granted complete precedence. We will see that such metaphysical-sounding problems tend to change appearances if we shed some of our naturalistic assumptions and "return," as the phenomenologists say, to our experience. Such a return has nothing mysterious or deeply metaphysical about it, but is simply a way of saying that experience may have a broader or different *meaning* than inherited paradigms allow. It is a way of being wary of our unquestioned presuppositions.

Lived time, the time of our lives, is obviously not devoid of meaning. It is not a mere succession of neutral now points, a formal grid transparent with respect to the content of experience. On the contrary, lived time seems to be in strict accord with the present meaning of experience. In other words, our sense of time changes with the significance of our experience. We live through "good times" and "bad times," we either "have the time" or we do not, though perhaps we can "make time." Our time—a time of indifference, a time of joy and hope, a time of despair—is bound not simply by a beginning and an end, but between what can more richly be described as "birth" and "death"; we do not end, we die. In this manner we could produce a catalogue of time (and times) that more closely respects its native meaning in our experience.

Of course we are still very likely to encounter the question "But what of time itself, that which we experience in this way?" But such a time is precisely not experienced; it exists for us as a concept only, like the theoretically precise units of atomic clocks that go their accurate way without us. Similarly, we indeed perceive the movements of the planets and of our sun and can generate a concept of time from them, but the time we are considering is the experiencing of such motions by human beings, not their movement per se. As Merleau-Ponty has said,

> Nothing will ever bring home to my comprehension what a nebula that no one sees could possibly be. . . . What, in fact, do we mean when we say that there is no world without a being in the world? Not indeed that the world is constituted by consciousness, but on the contrary that consciousness always finds itself already at work in the world.[1]

The nebula that gave birth to our solar system, the accuracy of clocks, these are both scientific conceptualizations and are experienced only as intellectual constructs deriving from our actual experience of the world, theoretically inferred from it perhaps. The point of this discussion is not, however, to doubt the efficacy of this scientific or naturalistic model, for it clearly produces important technological results.

But let us return to the question of identity. An analysis of temporality will reveal a continuity to conscious life. For the founder of phenomenology, Edmund Husserl, this life is linked through a continuous series of what he called temporal protentions (projections of a future) and retentions (consciousness of the immediate past) which give a density and cohesion to the ongoing present. William James expressed this same point rather well:

> the practically cognized present is no knife-edge, but a saddle-back, with a certain breadth of its own on which we sit perched, and from which we can look in two directions into time. The unit of composition of our perception is a *duration*. . . .[2]

This view of lived time (or experience) emphasizes its interlocked nature. The present transcends itself in a continual and unbroken anticipation of the future and retention of the past—as in the often cited experience of a musical melody. The various moments of a melody can be cognized as part of an ongoing melody only if our present consciousness is not cut off from the immediate past but includes it as constitutive of its present significance. It is this continuity, this duration, that is presupposed and demonstrated by any of our present actions. We do not need constantly to reformulate or consciously remember our initial rationale or desires to continue meaningfully a present action to its conclusion, for the projected end is part and parcel of the present act. It is because of this linked aspect of time that the present is meaningful in a way that punctual moments could never be.[3]

Our time consciousness, then, is fundamentally durational and not punctual. But there is a further important implication to this position which bears directly on the question of temporal continuity and identity. To return to Merleau-Ponty:

> The present still holds on to the immediate past without positing it as an object, and since the immediate past similarly holds its immediate predecessor, past time is wholly collected up and grasped in the present.[4]

It is precisely this phenomenon, this connectedness, that accounts for the experienced fluctuations of the "now" that we discussed earlier. The richness of the present is such that it discloses its horizons in accordance with the degree of penetration of our intentional gaze, and hence the degree of penetration required by our present task. We reach into the past in a fashion similar (I would not want to say the analogy is perfect) to the way our eyes penetrate the visual field—from the immediate vicinity to the far horizon—and concentrate on objects in the temporal field just as we might single out an object within the field of vision.

Apart from bodily identity, it is the above phenomenon of temporal connectedness that best accounts for our initial sense of personal identity; it certainly appears to be a necessary condition. At any moment we can become aware that the past (or a past) is accessible to us, is with us as ours. We are therefore also aware, though often only implicitly, that the past is tributary to the very meaning of the present. What should become clear here is that our link to a past is not something to be demonstrated, but is instead a given that all else is in various ways dependent upon. We would not wish, however, to conclude that all of one's life is therefore in theory redeemable—though this is the speculative conclusion of Bergson.[5] We would also not want to conclude that the past I am conscious of is *the* past as it actually was. We will have much more to say about this important problem later.

Let us now consider the human subject in relation to the above account of our lived time. So far we have seen that our temporal existence is characterized by what has been called (following Husserl) the "living present," a present that contains, as Augustine long ago pointed out in his *Confessions,* a present of things past and a present of things to come.[6] Consciousness, or awareness, is related to and caught up in this present in a dynamic fashion. Time is always my time; it is my life that gradually unfolds (along with the lives of others), and this unfolding is evidenced in my changing awareness, my changing states and developing possibilities. The movement of time is, we want to claim, nothing other than *subjectivity* furthering itself into its own possibilities.

"We must," said Merleau-Ponty, "understand time as the subject and the subject as time. . . . Time *is* someone."[7] If this co-constitution of the subject with time is correct, then it precludes or renders unnecessary the notion of a one-sided egological synthesis of time. That is, it precludes a founding subject peripheral or external to the stream of temporal genesis such as a transcendental ego.[8] Phenomenologically considered, the basic synthesis of time, and hence of the subject, is a passive synthesis (i.e., prior to self-conscious intentions) which, in an important sense, we ourselves are. It is at once something we effect (in living) and something that effects us as subjects. As Husserl has said, "The ego constitutes himself for himself in . . . the unity of a 'history' *(Geschichte).*"[9]

Husserl's remark signals the direction in which we have been heading. The overall temporal form of the subject's genesis is indeed historical. The unfolding of time is the unfolding of our history (our "story," as the German noun *Geschichte* also implies). The advantage of the term *history* over *temporality* is that it is less remote, in terms of ordinary language, from the actual content of experience. We generally think of history as comprising events and persons interacting, whereas temporality may easily be construed in abstraction from such events. Let us briefly consider how our history is generated at the level of passive constitution. I shall rely on Husserl's *Cartesian Meditations* for this brief but pertinent account.

Our consideration of the living present has shown that the present moment rides, as it were, on the immediate past and is also caught up in a futural project. This passive linking of the "now" with the "just passed" and the "just, just passed" (and so on) is already enough to found a temporal continuity for the subject. In the words of William James, "Each thought [moment of awareness] is born an owner, and dies owned."[10] But one need not think of this continuity as necessarily conscious. Consider Husserl's example:

> If, in an act of judgment, I decide for the first time in favour of a being and a being-thus, the fleeting act passes; but from now on *I am abidingly the ego who is thus and so decided*. . . . Likewise in the case of decisions of every other kind, value-decisions, volitional decisions.[11]

Such acts may well become determinants for my future actions, for it is on their basis that I adopt new beliefs and react in a certain characteristic way to a given state of affairs. They can be seen to constitute what Husserl calls an "abiding style" of my acts in the world; a form of predictability that he equates with a "personal character."[12] This character is thus constituted by a more or less unified and unifying substrate of habitualities or dispositions, of act types exhibiting a lawfulness determined by prior sedimented ego properties[13]—what in medieval thought was termed a *habitus*.

The habitus can usefully be seen, to borrow a phrase from Pierre Bourdieu, as "history turned into nature"; it is a past sedimented into "structuring structures."[14] Such habitual dispositions are formative in both mental and emotional life just as they are in the performance of manual skills, and as such they function in what can be called a passive or unconscious manner. On the broader societal level, the habitus has important functional similarities to the phenomenological concept of a prevailing, though very often unconscious or horizonal, life world *(Lebenswelt)* of sedimented values, beliefs, and attitudes, the unity of which must be accounted for by similar environmental conditions and prevailing cultural traditions.

The formation of a habitus, then, is the relatively abiding result of our temporal genesis, the result of acts reinforced by reactivation (*Reaktivierung* in the Husserlian sense) and repetition, but also the result of acts and decisions guided and often determined by a constraining social order and environment. One might also say, following Husserl, that one's habitus is the mediatory style of one's contact with the world, and that it generates a cultural world correlated to its structures. The typical style of my being-in-the-world is thus the dynamic equivalent of my habitus, and, as already noted, this habitus is very much the structural basis of my abiding character and also of my identity; this latter point is one we will come back to.

In the beginning of this chapter I stressed that temporality must not be viewed to the exclusion of the life that is temporal. Now, although we have seen this interweaving in action, there is still much that remains to be said concerning this life of ours. Of primary importance is the formation of self-consciousness and self-understanding as they fit into the above scheme. But so far we have barely left the level of what phenomenologists have called passive genesis, and much that has been said could in fact be taken to apply to the lives of chimpanzees as well as to humans. What I intend to investigate is, however, not simply the question of identity at this passive level, for I think that Husserl's and William James's analyses of lived time (to name but two attempts) are fairly adequate and convincing here, but the further constitution of the self—that "entity" for which David Hume could find no certain evidence and which is applied to monkeys only by way of analogy or through an act of personification.

Especially important for this task is an examination of the physical locus of our being-in-the-world (the body), and an examination of those important processes or events we roughly term mental—memory, imagination, emotion, and the like. But beyond these investigations stands another all-important phenomenon: language. Indeed, it is toward an understanding of language as it relates to our historical being and personal identity that our preliminary discussions are particularly oriented. We shall consider the role of embodiment in later chapters, for we should first consider, on the basis of the above analysis of time, that faculty which has, in the occidental philosophical tradition, been very closely related to the concept of personal identity: memory.

Memory and Recollection

> We live in memory and by memory, and our spiritual life is at bottom simply the effort of our memory to persist, to transform itself into hope . . . into our future.
>
> Miguel de Unamuno
> *Tragic Sense of Life*

It is perfectly understandable that memory is seen by many thinkers as somehow founding our experience of personal identity and selfhood. In acts of recollection I indeed seem to reactivate or at least contact in some important way moments of my past life, and I can also plot the general course of my life from a past moment up to the present, though often this is admittedly very sketchy. Our prior account of time was an attempt to explain why and how this recollection is, in the first place, possible.

To recapitulate briefly, the possibility for recollection arises from the cumulative horizonal structure of experience itself, what William James called "fringes." Past and future time can be grasped precisely because it is the still more or less operative horizon of the present; it is the context within which the present (e.g., perception) becomes meaningful, the background against which it makes sense for me. We have also seen how this accumulated horizon settles into a habitus which constitutes the more or less stable, more or less unconscious parameters of my acts in the world. This core accounts for the type or style of life that I lead, and therefore in some measure prescribes such things as the type of evaluations and judgments that I am now likely to make, and also the type of acts I am likely to perform.

What we call the past may, for our purposes, be considered in two primary ways. First there is the linear and objective view of a past stretching away irretrievably behind me, behind the present; the hours, the days, the years I have lived through, and even an interminable past before that. Second there is the more phenomenological-existential approach which makes of the present a being-in-the-world whose richness is inseparable from the *accumulated* significance of my successive experiences. This latter position is, in an important sense, more primordial because this constant awareness, this experienced weight of the past as it exerts influence in the present, grounds the more theoretical linear view and is in fact the experience the latter is derived from. In other words, without such a presence of the past we would probably not raise the question of past time itself. The linear view is an objective representation or recounting of lived time, and it posits a past, a history, that is irredeemably behind us, a past that is finished and which simply was as it was but is now gone. While we need not doubt the tautology that things were as they in fact were (remembering that they only were, in any meaningful sense, to certain observers or experiencers), it should be clear that now we have only recollections, artifacts, and nothing more. This loss of the past can only be remedied (made to accord with our experience) by a more existential and descriptive approach, one that actually allows us to make contact with and participate in the values of the past in the only way that seems possible, and, we should add, a way that is certainly not free from self-deception and falsity.

We have a present precisely because we are suspended in the network of our past (and impending future), and at any moment we may make this horizon thematic. As Merleau-Ponty has written concerning this experience,

> To remember is not to bring into the focus of consciousness a self-subsistent picture of the past; it is to thrust deeply into the horizon of the past and take apart step by step the interlocked perspectives until the experiences which it epitomizes are *as if* relived in their temporal setting.[15] (My emphasis.)

The past, as we have seen, is a dimension of our temporal being and is therefore potentially accessible not merely through static representations (discrete memory images, say) but also, and primarily, by extending or redirecting our awareness in the relevant "direction," e.g., away from the present praxis which we are caught up in or away from acts of pure fantasy. This process is, as it were, a movement through time that very often attempts to reconstruct a more or less coherent story of certain past events. But we shall see that this coherence is perhaps due more to what we feed into the material than the basic material of recollection itself. Memory images function more as tokens or traces for a certain intended sense than as the sole bearers of sense themselves. The material of recollection is analogous to archaeological finds that still require interpretation for their precise temporal location and sense.

What we must avoid here is the untenable position that such recollections are images which somehow duplicate original experiences, as though now we could relive them precisely as they once were. We tend very often blindly to assume recollection simply to be how things actually were in the past; this is the empiricist's storehouse of past and faded perceptions, a position that we find highly questionable. Such a traditional empiricist approach may be fine for knowledge claims ("knowing that" or semantic memory, e.g., "I know that I was there at 9:00 P.M."), but it is impossible to verify for claims relating to a supposed duplication of experience. Much of what we shall say here is in support of this latter rejection.

Memory, in what can be called its primary or immediate form (following Husserl), is already operative in perception. The very structure of the living present, containing what Husserl called futural *protentions* and also *retentions* of the immediate past, accounts for the continued identity of perceived entities and the objects of consciousness generally. It is difficult for us even to imagine living in a world wherein the present is cut off entirely from its immediate past! But if retention is part and parcel of present consciousness, then what we normally mean by the word *remembering* must be distinguished as a second form of memory. *Remembering,* or *recollection,* refers to acts which intend a content that is no longer an operative part of the living present.[16] One might call this form of recollection a re-presentation, but this term has strong connotations of a duplication of original experiences. I prefer to see remembering as operating with *representatives* of the past, where this concept may include symbols, schemes, or other tokens that can *stand for* the past. A fairly cursory glance at many of our everyday recollections (of people, places, events, etc.) will show just how sketchy and impoverished the material of recollection usually is; as a representation it would be very weak indeed, but as a representative it may be more than adequate.

This latter form of memory (and from now on I shall refer to the former type simply as retention) reaches its apex in what might be called occurrences of déjà vu—experiences of "then is now." An exemplar of this is the case of the madeleine cake described by Proust in the beginning of *Remembrance of Things Past.* Here we find not simply a knowledge that the past contained such-and-such an event, but also an imaginative "reliving" of the past in the temporal manner of the original experience (admitting that this can only be presumptive). Such a memory begins with a passive and somewhat brief flash of recollection that, because of its implied significance, prompts the experiencer to unpack, to narrate, the past that it refers to or seems to encapsulate. It is important to note here that in Proust's case this narrating is in fact a retrieval of the self.

There is, however, one condition built into memory, and this is the "nowness" of the "then," or the fact that memory implies a present act of recollection that is temporally distinct from the time which is recollected. If one has, in such an experience, lost the awareness of the present in which the recollection occurs, then one can no longer talk of memory but rather of hallucination, delusion, or some such state. For a state to be properly classed as memory, the experiencer must be able to separate the recollection from the present in which it is recollected. Sometimes it is only after the fact that we realize certain experiences we have been caught up in to consist primarily of memories; a similar phenomenon often occurs with dreams. Consciousness of something as memorial, then, presupposes there to be one time within another, past time within present time—rather as a story or novel may have both the time of the narrative and the time of the narrating. On the question of whether déjà vu presents the past as it actually was, there seems to be no possible way of proving it and much, as we shall see, that would lead us to doubt it.

The empiricist John Locke viewed memory as central to our experience of personal identity, but with little respect for the difference "now" makes to "then": "as far as any intelligent being can repeat the idea of any past action with the same consciousness it had of it at first, and with the same consciousness it has of any present action; so far is it the same personal self."[17] Memory in this ideal or veridical state would be the consciousness of a past stream of consciousness, one embedded in the other—the past relived from the standpoint of the present. As already noted, if you take away this present then you remove the point of comparison that is necessary for remembrance to be cognized as such. Certain dream states, for example, may indeed be little more than a rerun of certain of the day's events, but they usually attain their status as memorial from the perspective of a later comparative reflection.

The question concerning the veridicality of memory, however, is not cleared up by simply saying that the past is relived or remembered, for there is always the influence of the present perspective to contend with. Memorial experience (recollection) is not simply of the past; it is, as we have said, the past for me *now,* and this qualification makes a considerable difference. Perhaps, as Bergson thought, only in deep sleep do we minimize the influence of the present over the recollection, and this because there is very little guiding prejudice from our present praxis. But an important question to be considered here is the degree of infiltration of imagination into what is recollected.

Imagination is difficult to separate from memory because it shares a similar phenomenal structure. Their difference, where it is discernible, lies especially in the belief accompanying each presentation. In the case of recollection we acquiesce to its pastness because of such factors as familiarity, corroboration with other memories, and a certain involvement of ourselves in what is presented—it may, for example, revive a certain shame that we still feel in relation to the event. The experience of a past *as if* it were relived or as if "this is how it was" is often enough to draw us into a certain intimacy that may sometimes, though not always, be lacking from simply imaginative projections. However, as especially happens with memories from early childhood, an imaginative projection can easily settle into the gaps left vacant by recollection, such that we can no longer be certain of the difference between them. Imagination very often presents us with a past that we wish we had lived, or with the past as we now wish we had lived it. We might say, with Gaston Bachelard, that imagination augments recollection and the values of the memories recollected.[18]

What must now be addressed is the important question of personal identity as it relates to memory. We have seen from our earlier analyses how the possibility of memory is founded upon the retentional structure of temporality, but what of the subject whose past this is? We have already referred to Locke in the above account, and it will be useful to look a little further into his influential description of personal identity. What interests us is Locke's stress on the role of consciousness over against a substance-oriented account of personal identity. Locke writes, "Nothing but consciousness can unite remote existences into the same person: the identity of substance will not do it. . . ." He also says, "as far as . . . consciousness can be extended backwards to any past action or thought, so far reaches the identity of that person."[19] Personal identity, for Locke, is thus equal to my memorial grasp, equal to what I can now encompass of my past. This position ignores the passive sedimentation of the past into my habitual and unreflected attitudes and general world view (Locke's account is in terms of temporal expanse rather than density—horizontal rather than vertical), but it aligns well with cases of memory disorder and the loss or deformation of personal identity that can result from such a loss.

Although, as we have seen, habitus is history turned into nature and the past is therefore operative in the present, self-consciousness is another matter. My identity for myself is the identity I am conscious of, the identity I can bring to awareness. This identity is not necessarily something objective and pregiven that can simply be turned toward and noted (as though "I" were outside it); its nature is rather correlated to my interests and to the degree of penetration of my recollection, the expanse it surveys. In a certain sense this makes me responsible for my identity. One might talk, for instance, of Proust's identity being richer or broader than that of other people because he devoted a great deal of time to this recuperative act (assuming his major work to be primarily autobiographical). Let us now look further at this question of personal identity and its relation to recollection. We shall continue with Locke, then move on to Hume; both thinkers were among the first to address this question in depth.

Whereas the definition of *man* also takes account of physical or bodily identity, the definition of *person*, for Locke, relies primarily on a continuity of awareness. A person is "a thinking intelligent being, that has reason and reflection, and can consider itself as itself, the same thinking thing, in different times and places. . . ."[20] It is this identity over time and the contents encompassed by it that constitute, for Locke, our "self," and this therefore includes the consciousness of our own bodies.[21] What is important to note here is that our identity is independent of the normal changes in our body and principally dependent on consciousness and memory. For Locke, the resulting self, as we saw earlier, cannot be reduced to an entity or substance underlying identity. In this sense he was anti-Cartesian.

In not substantizing this self, Locke was criticized for giving ontological precedence to the "I think" (the "mental" process) rather than to the "I am" which is usually presupposed by it.[22] A remark by Bishop Butler, David Hume's contemporary, emphasizes this point: "One should really think it self-evident that consciousness of personal identity presupposes, and therefore cannot constitute, personal identity. . . ."[23] Locke's view, however, eschews such a (perhaps metaphysical-religious) supposition and relies solely on empirical observation. But it was Hume who reaped many of the results of Locke's position and provided a significant rebuttal to Butler.

It is common knowledge that Hume's empiricist epistemology demands that our knowledge claims rely on "impressions" (or perceptions) for their validation. This led to Hume's notorious repudiation of the "self":

> when I enter most intimately into what I call *myself,* I always stumble on some particular perception or other, of heat or cold, light or shade, love or hatred, pain or pleasure. I never can catch *myself* at anytime without a perception and never can observe anything but a perception.[24]

In thus rejecting the empirical evidence for an intuitively given (an "impression") and substantial soul, Hume ends in what might be called agnosticism. But having avoided this underlying metaphysical substance, he proceeds with the remaining and important task of explaining the nature and genesis of our belief (which he nevertheless admits exists) in personal identity.

Hume discovers certain relations operative on the flux of perceptions that create a sense of continuity across our impressions (perceptions), viz. resemblance, contiguity, and causation. For these categories to be effective, however, memory must already be in effect: "Had we no memory, we never shou'd have any notion of causation, nor consequently of that chain of causes and effects, which constitute our self or person."[25] Significant here, because different from Locke, is that although Hume also grounds personal identity on memory, he then proceeds to the notion of causation as the final phase in constituting this identity. This important move allows him to extend identity beyond the memory consciousness of Locke, and this by simply inferring back along a chain of causes that may no longer be intuitively given. The following remark can be taken as a criticism of Locke:

> will he affirm, because he has entirely forgot the incidents of these days, that the present self is not the same person with the self of that time; and by that means overturn all the most established notions of personal identity? . . . 'Twill be incumbent on those, who affirm that memory produces entirely our personal identity, to give a reason why we can thus extend our identity beyond our memory.[26]

This is an important point. It is indeed the case that we commonly extend our identity beyond explicit consciousness of past events, and we do this by a form of inference. There is, however, a point in Locke's favor that should be mentioned here, for what goes beyond explicit consciousness is only *thought to be,* it is a "remembering that" such-and-such occurred but without a recollected presentation or impression of the past experience; it is an inference only.

For Hume, imagination serves as the underlying synthetic activity that is indispensable for constituting the world as we know it, for it is imagination that grounds causality and the other relations. Memories are thereby knit into the fabric of our world, and they attain their status as memory largely through connectedness with other events known and recollected. An isolated image might, as we have said, easily be an hallucination or phantasm if it did not link into the broader network of memorial events that form our past life. Some type of causality is indeed at work here. How often have we said something of the form "No, I must have only seen it on television, because I know I was actually away in Europe at the time." Images are not memorial in and of themselves; they require a context, they require corroboration from related events to become meaningful or be meant in a certain way. Another way of saying this is that memory attains its important status as it links into and develops part of the story of our lives.

Memories are not what they are because they somehow mirror a pregiven and meaningful reality (Merleau-Ponty's "self-subsistent picture of the past"). Recollection, like perception, involves a considerable degree of interpretation; this is especially apparent in traditional psychoanalytic practice where the meaning of what is recollected may go through various stages of interpretation. Our access to what we call the past is guided by current interest, and the past is rarely if ever unfolded in the same way twice (though we may have, say, numerically the same visual images more than once).[27] To put this another way: the past is not always experienced as fixed, over and done with. The past only approaches "objectivity" when it is documented in some repeatable and accepted form, as in history books, for example. But the past may also become dogmatized to attain a fixed sedimented form in our own thoughts. Furthermore, what we regularly remember from the distant past is often just a repeatable token or icon taken for the real thing. Here we again link up with the notion of memory consisting of *representative* images and thoughts.

The kind of causality that Hume discusses is not far from the causality utilized in scientific praxis, where the relations are of logical and necessary connections: if A, then B. But what must not be forgotten with respect to such causal and logical investigations is that they are themselves carried out within a certain context; they are part of a larger program, part of a broader scientific narrative. To discover this narrative we must always be ready to ask, "But why is that result or that research important?" Our actions do not occur in a vacuum, but are woven into the fabric of an encompassing and often demanding praxial situation. The scientific narrative is what plots (no matter how vaguely) the nature and purpose of this situation.

Applying the above view to memory, we see that a similar configuration occurs. Beyond actual recollection I may rightly infer other events preceding or following that which I remember, events that are causally connected with it. But along with this mere recounting of events another type of "causality" is operative, one brought about by the demands of understanding. When a past state of affairs is reflected upon, a degree of *emplotment* is enacted. What this emplotment does is turn occurrences, discrete events or images, into moments in a narrative composition, and it is, I contend, this narrative structuration that most effectively generates our understanding of the past.

James Olney has said of autobiography that it has the power of "transforming the mere fact of existence into a realized quality and a possible meaning."[28] In this respect we can say that memories, or images we take to be memorial, are very often occasions for interpretation and narration, just as many perceptions also are. This is what we may usefully call the *hermeneutic* dimension of memorial awareness. To illustrate the above process we shall consider some examples taken from the work of Marcel Proust.

In Proust's writings we find many instances where a present perception will, through resemblance to something past, set off memorial reverberations or associations that promote the unfolding of a past drama, which may at first be purely passive. Proust in fact extols this passive dimension:

> Several summers of my life were spent in a house in the country. I thought of those summers from time to time, but they were not themselves. They were

> dead, and in all probability they would remain so. Their resurrection, like all these resurrections, hung on a mere chance.[29]

Intellect, he says, must be put aside in favor of those chance or involuntary sensations or objects that are a reservoir of the past's lived meaning and that may bring the past alive in a way that mere cognitive remembering cannot do.

Now although this account has a great deal of truth in it, it is surely not the whole story, as we will see. Proust himself does not stop his "reminiscences" at this point of chance encounters but goes on to unfold his past in great length and detail. The past, he says, may remain "captive forever [in the object], unless we should happen on the object, recognize what lies within, call it by its name, and so set it free."[30] Here we already see the need for a preliminary hermeneutics; we must both recognize and name: "Now and again, alas, we happen on an object, and the lost sensation thrills in us, but the time is too remote, we cannot give a name to the sensation, or call on it, and it does not come alive."[31]

The sensation, the image, it could even be a word, functions in the manner of a symbol that rings with potential meaning. We know there is a message here for us, but very often this situation is like encountering a person we have known and whose name now escapes us along with the relevant details of our acquaintance; we are frustrated at having forgotten, and no conversation ensues because we must turn away from the other to avoid embarrassment. The encounter with such images places a demand on us, a demand to be heard, to be deciphered. Perhaps this demand occurs because the deciphering is also, in effect, a retrieval of ourselves. This form of retrieval becomes more explicit in *Remembrance of Things Past:*

> One experiences, but what one has experienced is like those negatives which show nothing but black until they have been held before a lamp, and they, too, must be looked at from the reverse side; one does not know what it is until it has been held up before the intelligence. Only then, when one has thrown light upon it and intellectualized it can one distinguish—and with what effort!—the shape of what one has felt.[32]

If the past, then, is not to remain just a collection of vaguely intuited phantasms, it must undergo interpretation, and this is intellectual work. Memories, in what I take to be the primary sense of the term, are the result of such interpretation. This situation is somewhat like encountering a new metaphor. For a metaphor to be more than a mere novel figure of speech it must give rise to a new insight; it must imaginatively refigure or redescribe its object or resituate the subject it is addressed to. In the case of memory it is a question of reconstituting, as it were, the drama surrounding a certain imagined object or state of affairs (presumed to be from the past), which may likewise refigure the past and quite possibly also resituate the subject (in both a cognitive and emotional sense—as in Heidegger's notion of *Befindlichkeit*). The philosopher and poet George Santayana was very aware of this imaginative-reconstructive ingredient:

> When I remember I do not *look* at my past experience, any more than when I think of a friend's misfortunes I look at his thoughts. I imagine them; or rather I imagine something of my own manufacture, *as if I were writing a novel* and I attribute this intuited experience to myself in the past, or to the other person.[33] (My emphasis.)

The literary allusion is very important here, for it stresses the important narrational factor in remembrance. For Santayana the objects and events of our past are revivified through "moral imagination."[34] It is this latter ability that creates a dramatization characteristic of lived and hence valorized experience. As Santayana implies, it is the narrative result that we take to be the structure and import of our past lives. And it should be clear why novelists must become experts in this form of reconstitution if they are to present in their works something with the depth and dimensions of life itself.

A further factor to consider here is that, as we saw before, the past may be narrated in many ways. It is very easy to believe that the past is something irredeemably fixed and determined behind oneself, for in a certain sense this is true; objectively speaking, I have presumably been to certain places at certain times and have done certain ineradicable things. We have also seen from Husserl that the "I" is the abiding result of such acts. But there still remains the all-important question of the *meaning* of the past for me *now*.[35] I am not a machine that simply displays the past; I also respond to the display, and experience consists of both these factors at once. I may recall a definite datable event, I may even recall what that event meant to me at a prior date, but there is no necessary reason why this meaning should still be operative or important to me. In fact, even my recollection of what an event once meant to me will already be told from a new perspective, out of a new background, as part of a new narrative.

Our accounts of the past can only be expected to have a degree of consistency if they are written down or are remembered and retold frequently. This is, for example, the practice in many religious groups where the dogmas are recited regularly. It is also present in compulsives where an event (possibly traumatic) is obsessively run through again and again. But there is an incipient stagnation in all such enterprises, as Nietzsche well knew. In the language of Rudolf Bultmann, the kerygma must be interpreted anew for a new age, a new world view. The change such reinterpretation brings about is, we have been arguing, natural to human understanding and development.

What we cannot escape in the case of recollection is Gadamer's hermeneutic principle of "effective history" (*Wirkungsgeschichte*). We are finite historical beings whose understanding is mediated by and made possible through our history. We have no transcendental standpoint from which the past may be seen without the interference of "subjectivity" (the present). This means that there never was such a pristine or finished meaning to the past; a supposedly "true" meaning that we ought now to recapture or coincide with, that we might once and for all pin down. In matters of the past we cannot escape the historicity of our gaze and our interests. However, this position need not lead to a total relativism where anything goes, where any interpretation will do, for the past we would recapture is woven into the same fabric that guides our understanding. As Bultmann has also stressed, "The subjectivity of historians does not mean that they see falsely, but only that they choose certain perspectives and proceed by way of asking questions."[36] We cannot avoid this perspectivism if we seek to understand and not merely repeat by blind rote or chronicle. It is a trait of a naive objectivism to believe that events have, or had, a univocal meaning which constitutes the "truth" of those events. The past, on the contrary, and if our analyses are correct, should be viewed as part of our lives, and because life is unfinished so is the meaning of the past.

What now becomes crucial for our endeavor is to consider further the narrational and interpretive aspects of recollection, especially with a view to grasping the implications this has for personal identity and selfhood. So far little has been said about the self, the subject who recollects, and it is interesting just how much can be said about memory without having to analyze this mysterious "entity." The self is nevertheless intimately bound to most of our conceptions of memory and recollection. The kind of continuity that pertains to memory has usually been linked with the kind of continuity that is required by a notion of self and especially of self-identity. It is also, we often say, to a particular self that the various memories accrue; I am their owner, as it were.

Beyond this is what we may call the motivator position, which maintains that "I" remember, that "I" think. Here we find the self as an agent, as an instigator of acts. While it must be admitted that we do indeed say "I think," "I remember," and so on, there has been a troubled history surrounding the ontological status of this "I." What interests us here is the degree to which our talk of the self is self-constituting rather than referential to an ontologically prior subject. The next chapter will go part way toward answering, in a broad fashion, some preliminary questions concerning the self, particularly the self's implication in the narratives and practices of our life-world.

II

ON NARRATIVE

Our lives are ceaselessly intertwined with narrative, with the stories that we tell and hear told, those we dream or imagine or would like to tell, all of which are reworked in that story of our own lives that we narrate to ourselves in an episodic, sometimes semiconscious, but virtually uninterrupted monologue.

Peter Brooks
Reading for the Plot

To raise the question of the nature of narrative is to invite reflection on the very nature of culture and, possibly, even on the nature of humanity itself.

Hayden White
"The Value of Narrativity in the Representation of Reality"

The accounts of personal identity given by empiricists such as Locke and even by Husserl in his more radical approach are adequate as a basis, a starting point. The problem for us with such views is their foundational bias, their desire to explain a phenomenon by resorting to primitive structures of consciousness and their operation; for Locke the cogito and the extent of our consciousness of the past, and for Husserl the fundamental temporal connectedness of lived time. Such a maneuver is like describing a house only in terms of its underlying framework, its skeletal structure; this really shows only the possibility of a house. Personal identity is not so easily guaranteed, and human reality, in all its richness and diversity, not that easily grasped or accounted for.

Already we have seen how imagination plays an important role in recollection, and as we proceed the influence of social reality and the linguistic and semiotic systems (e.g., language, gestures, literature) on which it depends will become equally important. Our task now is to pursue further the nature of narrative and the important relation it bears to our lives. The previous chapter already takes us some distance in this direction. At this point we will not be discussing narrative in its literary dimensions but will concentrate on narration and narrative structures as they pertain to experience generally.

It is, I shall maintain, the narrated past that best generates our sense of personal identity, and the emphasis is on the word *personal* because emplotment may indeed create the individual meaning or story of our lives for ourselves. Narration into some form of story gives both a structure and a degree of understanding to the ongoing content of our lives. Clearly, personal identity implies more than an empty pole of identity and more than just temporal continuity. What makes personal identity personal is that it is *my* characteristic identity, *my* particular life with all its turns and vagaries. We have already begun to see a link between self-understanding and narrative—that persons gain at least some of their meaning through the story of their past (this can be extended in a like manner to their future)—and, as I hope to show, the meaning of a life can be adequately grasped only in a narrative or storylike framework.

I will begin by briefly considering the nature of our sense of self (myness), a theme continually returned to and developed throughout the book. The next section will consider the implicit and explicit narrative structure of our experience, and will introduce the important problem of expression. The third section serves to illustrate the narrative position through a consideration of the higher emotions and their dependence on language. Finally, we will consider the importance of narrative in ethics and value theory.

"I Am I."

That "I am I" seems not to be doubted (outside philosophy!). I am myself and no other. I wake from a troubled dream and soon continue into the day as my old self. "I am I"—how secure and indubitable that sounds, and as a performative assertion of identity it has served and continues to serve us very well. Indeed, how could I not believe in myself! Even the wildly decentered and disoriented character in Beckett's *The Unnameable* asserts it against everything to the contrary: "I can't go on, I must go on." Of course, our ordinary parlance has the result of promoting the belief in a substantial self behind, as it were, such utterances as "I am speaking," "he looks that way," and so on. It may also promote the belief that this self is potentially knowable, an *object* of knowledge that can, say, be brought forward or mirrored in language. In this way we unwittingly generate the problematic and metaphysically tinged subject that a narrative theory seeks to circumvent. We say "I" as though referring to an active or motivating subject ontologically prior to the action, underlying it (a sub-stance). As Nietzsche stated the matter, "The separation of the 'deed' from the doer . . . this ancient mythology established the belief in cause and effect after it had found a firm form in the functions of language and grammar."[1]

Thus, when Descartes discovered his first principle, the *ego cogito,* he was led to assert thereby that the I spoken of existed (in some sense) prior to the pronouncement, outside the discourse (and outside the *Discourse On Method*!). We end up with the well-known Cartesian substantial dualism, something that is not well supported by our ordinary experience or modes of comprehension. It is especially the reification and mystification implicit in this Cartesian subject that a narrative account (and perhaps postmodern thought in general) seeks to avoid. This substantial self, I contend, is no more (nor less) than a fiction, which is, in a sense that will become clearer, all the self can ever be. As an *implied subject*—implied, that is, from acts of expression—the self is a social and linguistic construct, a nexus of meaning rather than an unchanging entity.

Now, the saying of "I" may be an act of repetition, but that it repeats the same self over time can be considered an artful illusion, one reason being that more often than not it is empty of content—in much the same way that Hegel considered Fichte's self-identical ego to be empty of content. We shall see later that the saying of "I" is not a simple referential and designatory utterance in the way saying "this dog" or "that lamp" can be. "I" may also be devoid of significance or informative content; it is not like saying "English" or "extravagant." When we are asked what "I" refers to, a common answer is the tautological-sounding "me"! I would claim, on the contrary (and assuming that the statement in fact had a specific sense), that the *I* does not even coincide with itself; such coincidence is perhaps an unattainable and misguided goal. This point was already prefigured in our discussion of the unavoidable interpretive dimension of memory.

Between consciousness and itself is a certain otherness (an alter ego) that, in an Hegelian *Aufhebung,* has to be integrated, reconciled with itself. But there is a delay here, a noncoincidence. It is not as though self-consciousness accumulates, expands, or builds up further what it already was, reaching an apex in self-transparency. The Hegelian story is that of a changing habitus, or a changing tradition, where each stage has its attendant sense of self and reality. But it is more than this, for each stage has a certain forgetfulness of its predecessors.[2] The "I" of today is not necessarily the "I" of tomorrow.

We see that the mere saying of "I" tells us very little about identity and continuity, though it does seem to presuppose them, or at least beg the question of them. The important question to ask someone who says "I" is very often "who?" rather than "what?"—sometimes we ask it of ourselves.

Unlike much of philosophy, which often contents itself with the question of *what* a self is, we must turn toward literature and narrative to learn more concerning *who* the self is.

Hannah Arendt has particularly stressed the difference between who and what a person is. The latter question is answered, she says, in terms of attributes and qualities (brain surgeon, engineer, brave, thoughtful, intuitive, etc.), but these are properties that one may share with numerous other individuals; this approach overlooks individuality.

> *Who* somebody is or was we can only know by knowing the story of which he is himself the hero—his biography, in other words; everything else we know of him, including the work he may have produced and left behind, tell us only *what* he is or was.[3]

Arendt illustrates her case by alluding to the interesting fact that we know *who* Socrates was even though we have no actual works of his, whereas the same cannot be said, at least not to the same degree, of Plato or Aristotle. (That one leaves behind an autobiographical work must surely cause us to amend Arendt's position to some degree. Her argument, however, stresses the whole of a life, and in that case an autobiography cannot possibly be final.)

Properties, as ordinary language suggests, are indeed attributes of someone, of a particular self. But this individual is not the self of some direct introspective scrutiny; it is rather the self of a personal history, of a narrated life. In narrating the acts of an individual we contribute to the creation of that individual as a definite *character.* As Alasdair MacIntyre has written, "The self inhabits a character whose unity is given as the unity of a character." This character must therefore be considered in light of a story it belongs to. As MacIntyre also says, "characters in a history are not a collection of persons, but the concept of a person is that of a character abstracted from a history."[4] Another way of stating this initially counterintuitive view is that persons are such only if (among other things) they can be considered to have a history, a history of acts and involvements. We may use the term *person* without knowing that history, but a history is nevertheless always implied.

One reason, presumably, why automatons can be excluded from the category of personhood is because they have no comparable history for themselves. But the manufacture of automatons with some form of memory implant could cause problems for this categorization. The widely known science fiction film *Bladerunner* is especially informative in this respect, for it poses in a striking way the problem of the *experiential* similarity of implanted versus real memories. In such a case we may well ask, if one cannot tell the difference between implanted and real memories should this affect our predication of personhood? This problem has clear similarities to the often cited question raised by Russell. If the universe were actually created only a second ago, and we sprung into being fully equipped with memories that appear to date from years back, could we ever know the truth of our genesis? It seems not.

Persons not only have memories, histories, but also take certain attitudes toward them. We notice change—that things and acquaintances are not as they once were. We may enjoy the intimacy of our memories. We show concern over what we remember having done. We despair about losing memories in old age. Factors such as these also contribute to our category of personhood. Now if the attitude of the supposed automaton toward its "memories" is that it simply views them as so much data, then again we may be wary of predicating personhood. There is, perhaps, no single criterion for ascribing personhood to something, and on some of the criteria it may be very difficult to decide one way or the other.

Along similar lines, analytic philosophers are fond of discussing the nature of persons through hypothetical examples of a science fiction sort. Derek Parfit, for example, begins the discussion of personal identity in his book *Reasons and Persons* by considering the case of someone who is teleported to a distant planet.[5] This operation consists of some form of encoding of the person's total being and the transmission of these data for reconstitution at another location. The person is of course then totally decomposed at the original location. It must be admitted that while such an example is purely hypothetical, consideration of it may nevertheless reveal important assumptions about our notion of personhood. We might be led to think that the person simply continues his existence at the other location. But suppose the decomposition did not occur; do we then have two persons or one? There is certainly no numerical identity. Is the decomposition at the first site simply the death of that person? Is the other person therefore to be described as a duplicate, a copy? Should we feel guilt, supposing the decomposition did not work, if we had to destroy this duplicate, especially if it is qualitatively identical? Or, more radically, suppose it was you they forgot to decompose at the first site—would you happily be annihilated some time shortly after the transportation? Unless there were some form of "mental" communication or connection between the two, it would seem that they are now two different persons, or soon will be as their lives unfold in different directions.

The question of guilt takes us back to the automaton example. We have fabricated an individual that is identical to other persons, except in respect of having actually lived its past. Whether this latter fact counts against its being a person is very much a matter of our social conditioning and our traditions, our way of understanding. If we reject the onto-theological notion of a soul substance, then presumably other criteria, such as social responsibility, social interaction, and perhaps even procreation, must gain importance, especially if bodily differences do not play a significant role. It is, however, not my aim in this work to address such empirical and hypothetical questions directly other than to show how they may problematize our standard conceptions of identity and personhood.

While we are on the topic of identity, we should say a word or two about Neurath's ship. Is a ship still the same craft if during a voyage all its planks are gradually replaced by new ones? There is an obvious analogy here to persons, whose cells change considerably during the course of their lives. What is perhaps best asked in such examples is why the issue is difficult to decide. We tend to waver between yes and no on such questions. If we replace a few planks, we tend to think of the boat as the same. If the planks were of a different shape we may think the boat to be different. If the planks were all replaced during one afternoon, we may think it is now a new ship, though from a legal point of view it may still be registered as the same vessel. Coming back to our previous example, two identical ships would not, other than very loosely, be considered the same ship.

The problem here is that our notion of identity is not always a clear-cut matter. We allow for identity in difference. After each use the ship changes, and from year to year so do we. Things change in time, and our notion of identity seeks to find some continuity in this change. Legally, for example, we are considered the same person throughout our lives. But it is conceivable that with the rise, say, in organ transplants the issue of identity could become quite problematic. What this identity or continuity consists in is often relative to the type of entity considered, and relative to the reasons one has for positing identity. Let us now return from this digression and continue our consideration of narrative.

It is no accident that the word *person* derives from the Latin *persona,* which has connotations of a character in a play. According to our historically oriented position, the full characterization of who someone is must wait until the action reaches completion, until the play is finished (if it ever is!). This is why Arendt claims that "action reveals itself fully only to the storyteller, that is, to the backward glance of the historian, who indeed always knows better what it was all about than the participants."[6] Presumably, however, the actor can become his or her own storyteller.

What is required here is an ability to extricate or distance oneself from embeddedness in the action and perceive it in the manner of a plot, a history. We often do this when a certain episode of one's life has reached a (perhaps temporary) conclusion. Though, of course, that our lives have episodes is very often the result of narrative acts that may occur well after the events in question and from a broader perspective than was possible in the past. This is the basis of Arendt's position.

Perhaps in a Sartrean sense we can say that only when our lives are finished (at death) is our essence complete, and perhaps from a god's all-encompassing perspective this essence then receives its final meaning. But from a human and hermeneutical point of view this meaning has a considerable margin of flux, for the story of a life can be told in a number of ways; we cannot help but be selective. We may admit, however, that the "truth" is more or less established in people's minds when a *version* of the story becomes generally accepted, becomes canonical. We often have such a great desire for the so-called truth that we will overlook its status as a version. Just as we change week by week, year by year, so do our narrations of the past.

The "I" does not fully coincide with itself—this is implied in Arendt's "backward glance" of the storyteller. Who I am is very often perceived (narrated) by others more clearly than by myself.[7] Perhaps we should say that there is my story of myself and there are numerous others, some of them from a vantage point superior to my own; consider our epistemic superiority to children as an example.

It may also be the case that the question of who I am often does not arise, and certainly not with any degree of urgency. Why this may be so is not difficult to fathom. One becomes locked into a mode of life that may not change in any essential way for many years. We repeat the same routines. One's habitus, that fund of practical but implicit and corporeal wisdom, is like an ocean upon which our personal consciousness floats, and where even this consciousness is but a part of that same ocean. One's home life, one's work and leisure may enter a routine pattern that one becomes implicitly identified with. If one is at home with and immersed in this life, then the question of "who?" need not arise. We are supported by our ongoing practices, our established meanings. It is often in light of a possible or impending future, or a problem in the present that the question of "who?" is seriously raised. In Proust's case, for example, we find the desire to perpetuate himself in writing in face of the immanent demise of his physical being and in light of his belief that no part of himself will survive, in a religious sense, this death of his body.

The meaning of my existence can also be a casual thing, fulfilled in the moments of my day-to-day praxis. My self-conception can be shallow and brief, or it can become my overriding concern (as it was for Proust). This variation also applies, of course, to other persons' conceptions of me. And am I anything other than these various conceptions, these versions, these stories told by and about us?

We see from the above that a good case can be made for distinguishing between what has been called, with relation to literature, the experiencing self and the narrating self.[8] Generally speaking, in self-understanding the narrating self is always trying to coincide with, or be adequate to, the experiencing self, but this path is easily frustrated or becomes a matter of self-deception. One must first have the means or vocabulary for expression, but then there is the perception of what material is relevant, the choice of when an episode begins and when it ends, the mode or genre of the expression, and numerous other details that can cloud the conversion. We will look at some of these questions in what follows, and especially at the nature of what I have called our prenarrative experience.

The Story of Our Lives

We will now consider in more detail the relation between narrative, time, and experience. For our present purposes, narration can be conceived as the telling (in whatever medium, though especially language) of a series of temporal events so that a meaningful sequence is portrayed—the story or plot of the narrative. It is the nature of a plot, traditionally considered, to synthesize events into a meaningful temporal whole, which it does by some form of closure or completion and by its developmental followability—that is, by giving a beginning, middle, and end structure to the narrative.[9] Such closure is effected through the resolution (sometimes partial or failed) of aporias that arise in earlier narrative stages. To narrate, then, is to tell the story or history of something or someone and usually involves human or anthropomorphic characters (actors) whose lives are in some respect exhibited.[10] Narrative, furthermore, generally implies the presence of a narrator who is the storyteller, though this may be a covert telling. This latter point is what generally distinguishes narrative from drama.[11]

Before proceeding, a few explanatory remarks are in order concerning my use of the terms *narrative* and, more importantly, *prenarrative* in relation to the human subject. In self-narration the narrator is commonly found in the first-person singular ("I then went to study at university . . ."), and what is related is the life of the narrator. In fact, in spoken autobiographical discourse the character, the narrator, and the author are assumed to be one and the same. Only when the listener suspects falsity or deception will he distinguish between them, particularly between the character portrayed and the author-narrator.[12] With regard to the subject matter of our personal narratives, the thematic material generally relates back, directly or indirectly, to what we are calling the prenarrative aspects of experience. The prenarrative is, in its most general form, the drama we call our lives. As dramatic, our lives cannot always be said to have a narrator, for it is only when, from within the drama, we take up the narrator's role that the story of our lives is actually told. Earlier, however, I defined this prenarrative as a quasi-narrative, implying that narration has already entered into it. This is indeed the case, for, as I hope to demonstrate in this chapter, we are constantly adopting the narrator's position with respect to our own lives and also the lives of others.

If, as we have seen, time is fundamentally the time of my life (between birth and death), personal identity will depend upon the continuity of meaningful experience in this life. The physical body may well be the permanent locus of my insertion in the world, and it is indeed a fairly solid basis for continuity, but it is the events that unfold from this locus that generate the meaning of my existence, both through the habitualities it embodies and the history it exhibits. Our lives are not experienced as random unconnected events (though they may be thought so upon reflection), and rarely as a series of such events. Actions are, generally speaking, already understood in the context of a before and after. Life is inherently of a narrative structure, a structure that we make explicit when we reflect upon our past and our possible future.[13]

The actions of human agents, to be intelligible, must be seen against the background of a history, a history of causes and goals, of failures, achievements, and aspirations. As MacIntyre writes, "The notion of a history is as fundamental as the notion of an action. Each requires the other."[14] Actions do not occur in a void and are not meaningful in and of themselves; their meaning is dependent on the broader perspective of a framing story, as events in a history.[15] We must ourselves know such a personal history if we are to make intelligent choices in the present.

It is a throughgoing characteristic of our lives that we view our actions as either beginning something (as a means) or as the conclusion of something. Practical reason itself shares this teleological structure of paths to envisioned goals. As Ricoeur states the matter, "An event is not only an occurrence, something that happens, but a narrative component."[16] I would further maintain that this particular narrative way of sequentializing is basic to the process of human understanding, especially as this is directed to acting, social persons. To understand a life is to trace its development upon a narrative thread, a thread that unites otherwise disparate or unheeded happenings into the significance of a development, a directionality, a destiny. We might again turn to Ricoeur: "The ability to follow a story constitutes a very sophisticated form of understanding."[17] That one is or becomes unable to do this for oneself will therefore promote the psychological consequence of our possibly experiencing a lack of development, of unity, and of directionality. We shall return to this conclusion in more detail when we look at some facets of contemporary psychoanalysis.

Time and memory, as I presented them in the preceding chapter, do not themselves constitute personal identity; they rather serve as the environment from which narrative structuration is possible. Explicit narratives are, one might say, of a higher order than the elements of temporality and memory from which they are usually woven, and it is this order that we need to explore in what follows.

It is as a character in our (and other people's) narratives that we achieve an identity. Ricoeur has made the same point:

> Our own existence cannot be separated from the account we can give of ourselves. It is in telling our own stories that we give ourselves an identity. We recognize ourselves in the stories that we tell about ourselves. It makes very

> little difference whether these stories are true or false, fiction as well as verifiable history provides us with an identity.[18]

Implied in this statement is that the self is generated and is given unity in and through its own narratives, in its own recounting and hence understanding of itself. The self, and this is a crucial point, is essentially a being of reflexivity, coming to itself in its own narrational acts.

This conclusion can be seen as an important outcome of Ricoeur's basic hermeneutic stance: "there is no self-knowledge without some kind of detour through signs, symbols and cultural works, etc."[19] Who I am is not given outside of such mediated expression. But, as we shall come to see, this is a case of expression creating being and not merely reporting or mirroring it after the fact. The self is not some precultural or presymbolic entity that we seek simply to capture in language. In other words, I am, for myself, only insofar as I express myself.

We might, however, still ask about experience itself, prior to being narrated. What is prenarrative experience? Is it not perhaps falsified when narrated? Does language impose its own cultural forms of expression on this stratum? There have been varying views on this topic. On one extreme is the influential position of Louis Mink: "Stories are not lived but told. Life has no beginnings, middles, or ends. . . ."[20] Thus if life has any narrative structure, claims Mink, it is one we have put there after the fact. He continues: "We do not dream or remember in narrative . . . but tell stories which weave together the separate images of recollection. . . . So it seems truer to say that narrative qualities are transferred from art to life." For Mink, storytelling is a mode of comprehension (of grasping together) that necessarily takes second place in relation to the experiences comprehended.

On the other extreme we find MacIntyre: "we all live out narratives in our lives and . . . we understand our own lives in terms of the narrative that we live out. . . ."[21] For MacIntyre narratives are inextricable from experience. Barbara Hardy, the literary theorist, also argues in this manner: "We dream in narrative, day-dream in narrative, remember, anticipate, hope, despair, believe, doubt, plan, revise, criticize, construct, gossip, learn, hate, and love by narrative."[22] The disagreement between Mink and MacIntyre can perhaps be resolved if we consider the relation between implicit and explicit narratives, though much of what I have so far said should discredit Mink's absolute severing of narrative from experience. We have already noted, for example, the narrational nature of recollection and the way temporality assumes a historical form linked to our purposes. Ricoeur is, I think, more rigorous in his analysis of the question of the relation between narrative and experience than either Mink or MacIntyre; his analysis can in fact serve to locate the other views more precisely.

Ricoeur's stance is in certain respects intermediary, though admittedly sometimes ambiguous. Narration is the imaginative act that configures a more primordial experience into something with meaning and structure: "the plots that we invent help us to shape our confused, formless and in the last resort mute temporal experience."[23] This sounds extremely close to Mink. More recently, however, Ricouer maintains that this primordial experience has a "prenarrative quality" or prefiguredness that "constitutes a demand for narrative."[24]

His current position can best be summed up by an opening remark from the first volume of *Time and Narrative*:

> Time becomes human time to the extent that it is organized after the manner of a narrative; narrative, in turn, is meaningful to the extent that it portrays the features of temporal experience.[25]

Let us try to unpack this quotation. Human time, as we saw from Husserl, is not the bare temporality of succession; it is a succession that already has various imports for the individual(s) concerned—it already has "features." We have already remarked that time is cut through with human values ("good times," "bad times," etc.), and in that time is already keyed to our purposes and therefore valorized, it must have been experienced in a contextualized form. For example, the present is "good" because something has turned out or is turning out well. Already there is in experience an implicit narrative structure and hence understanding. Our explicit narratives may indeed extend, even change, the meaning of our lived time, but this time is already structured according to our style of being-in-the-world, our habitus. As such, our narrative interpretations do not function ex nihilo but follow naturally upon the structure of experience.

If the temporality of human affairs is indeed experienced at its basic level within a teleological setting, then it is perhaps only narrative understanding that can do it justice. To narrate oneself is to make explicit this prenarrative or "prefigured" (Ricoeur) quality of our unexamined life, to draw out a story it embodies. This is to say that our unexamined life is already a quasi-narrative, and that lived time is already a drama of sorts. Also, and this is quite important, this quasi-narrative can and does serve as a corrective or guide for the act of narration. One cannot tell just any old story without committing some form of injustice to the content of one's experience—what Sartre called "bad faith." As David Carr has written,

> Many of our plans go awry (and stories have to be rewritten) because we make mistakes about the past, about what happened and what we have done. The past does constrain us; it does have a fixedness that allows reinterpretation only up to certain limits.[26]

Lived time already has a quasi-narrative character, and this is why it is not amenable to just any telling. One fabricates one's past at one's own risk—at the risk of one's self. Involved in such narrations can be both psychologically harmful factors associated with self-deception and repression and socially harmful ones associated with lying to and deceiving other people.

While Ricoeur does not go as far as I would like on the question of the quasi-narrative character of lived experience, he certainly goes partway. In the end he is willing (against Mink) "to accord already to experience as such an inchoate narrativity that does not proceed from projecting, as some say, literature on life but that constitutes a genuine demand for narrative."[27] This is an interesting intermediary position. Ricoeur is not saying experience lacks a narrative structure, but he is also not saying it always has a fully developed or explicit one. The point, if I am correct in my interpretation, is that experience naturally goes over into narration, which is very different from saying that narrative structures are *imposed* on experience. We have here a dialectic of the preexpressed and the expressed, where neither party is alien to the other. Narratives, for Ricoeur, are justified by the felt need for the untold *stories* of our lives to be told,[28] though he is, I believe, overly cautious and too brief in his discussion of this point. Such caution leads Carr, for example, to assimilate Ricoeur, wrongly in my opinion, to the camp of Mink. Our own position seeks to draw out the details and implications of what we see to be Ricoeur's middle position. It might be helpful at this point to take a brief look at some relevant aspects of Ricoeur's project in *Time and Narrative.*[29]

The three volumes of *Time and Narrative* are concerned with articulating the important and often overlooked role that emplotment plays in our experience of temporality. Its effect, much like that of metaphor in Ricoeur's earlier work, is the refiguration of experience. Emplotment, in histories and fictions, takes a prefigured world of events and actions and draws out or proposes a configuration that serves to organize worldly events into meaningful sequences and purposes. This textual structure is in turn the mediating cause of the reader refiguring his or her own world in light of the possibilities offered by experiencing the world of the text. The progression from prefigured to configured and refigured receives a technical elaboration in *Time and Narrative* in terms of three stages of mimetic representation: mimesis_1 (the everyday world of action), mimesis_2 (the stage of creative narrative configuration), and mimesis_3 (the appropriation of the work of mimesis_2 to the world of the reader).

These three inseparable mimetic levels serve to define the genesis of a human time which, claims Ricoeur, "is nothing other than narrated time" (3:102). This narrated time is reducible to neither cosmological (or objective) time nor subjective time (as explored by Husserl) but generates an additional and synthetic dimension to our temporal experience. Especially notable here is the historicization of our horizon of experience by the narrative work of historians. Narrative for Ricoeur, be it historical or fictional, involves a "search for concordance [that] is part of the unavoidable assumptions of discourse and communication" (2:28). Narration draws a figure out of the materials of everyday life but only, finally, in order that the story it unfolds returns back to and reconfigures that life. It is this point that is central to our above discussion. Narration should not be seen as creating order where there once was pure chaos or dissonance (1:72). Mimesis$_2$ configures what was already *prefigured,* and is not only a creative act but also one of discovery (2:76). The level of mimesis$_1$ already has a considerable degree of narrative structuration that allows actions to be viewed within a purposive and historical dimension. This structuration becomes even more apparent if we consider the point mentioned above, that mimesis$_3$ feeds back into the life-world of the reader, for structuration at the level of mimesis$_1$ is very much the product of earlier configurative acts that have been appropriated by the individual or taken on by society in general.

One has only to consider the remark "Traditions are essentially narratives" (3:260) to see the pervasiveness for Ricoeur of narrative structure at the level of everyday experience. This is not, however, to claim that we maintain a continual consciousness of the traditions we are embedded in, only that they have a certain intelligibility and a history that could be discovered and articulated; that is why we have used the term quasi-narrative for this domain. In what follows we shall pursue some further aspects of the relevance of narrative and narration to ordinary life.

Narration of oneself, because of the quasi-narrative character of ordinary life, may be both a receptive and a creative activity. If we turn to recollection we can clearly see a receptive and an active stage. Receptively our memories may already generate a broken narrative of images and meaning as they first enter conscious awareness. Often we do not have cause to notice just how broken and incomplete this recollection can be, for the fragments may nevertheless exhibit a quasi-narrative or dramatic structure that satisfies our need for meaning. (The same phenomenon may apply to dreams. No matter how disjointed, fragmented, or plain crazy the dream may be to later reflection, during the dream there is very often a definite sense of a plot unfolding.) But, as was earlier stressed, interpretation is inherent to recollection, and already this fragmented and schematic narrative is being filled out with a present meaning, is *configured* for me now.

Interpretation, like understanding, is a continuous process with no precise starting point. We cannot say of recollection that here is the bare content, and here is where interpretation and meaning start.[30] This situation is a primary problem for those who would maintain with Mink that there is experience on one hand and narrative interpretation on the other. Rather, interpretation has always already started.

Life, with a minimum of explicit narrative, approaches a sheer undergoing, like a child who does not consciously link A to B as it lives through them. This need not be William James's "confusion," for habitualities, motor actions, and our general life-style can serve us well as far as implicit structure is concerned, but the broader significance of one's experiences might thereby be unformed or lost—as indeed much of one's childhood is. We might now ask: but where does this broader significance reside? The answer can only be that it is generated through the narrative act itself. This important creative component is often overlooked. To narrate is to link A to B, to see causal affinities, to draw out and develop comparisons and harmonies, to deduce and project possible outcomes. As Ricoeur says, "To make a plot is already to make the intelligible spring from the accidental, the universal from the singular, the necessary or the probable from the episodic."[31]

Whereas the young child does not set out to consciously narrate but only runs through sequences of images (basic memory retrieval, or Piaget's picture consciousness), adults are *already* well initiated into a broad semiological realm. We already have language, we have been told stories, we have seen and read them; we are therefore no longer innocent in this respect. Our world is a progressively cultural one, where even nature is a cultural concept with a varying history. To quote Ricoeur once more: "We belong to history before telling stories or writing history. The game of telling is included in the reality told."[32] This is a very important insight, one that backs up our earlier interpretation of Ricoeur's position on narrative. We might say that we are "story-telling animals" precisely because we are already caught up in a story, and already committed to meaning.

One reason we narrate is because mankind cannot fail at times to ask the question of its own being, because we know the story is there to be told—just as others have told it. But there is also, as Ricoeur stresses, the desire to make the inchoate intelligible, and we know that narrative understanding is traditionally suited to this task, as literature clearly shows. Our point in arguing for a quasi-narrative level is precisely that "telling is included in the reality told." We are both experiencers and narrators (often pretty much at the same time), for the act of making intelligible is a more or less continuous one, even though the narratives may be appropriated from elsewhere. It is this continuity of our life story that constitutes the greater part of our experienced self-identity. Our identity is that of a particular historical being, and this identity can persist only through the continued integration of ongoing experience. Because we bring our history along with us, as a more or less clearly configured horizon, new experiences will tend to flow into this story of our lives, augmenting it and adapting themselves to it.

At the broadest and most abstract level this identity is constituted out of the part-whole relation between the "now" and the at least implicit horizon of my life as a whole. The mere fact of situating the now within such a frame is already enough to generate an identity, and one need not know much about the life itself for this relation to operate. Let us consider an example. You are listening to a piece of music at a concert. Even though you may not be able to identify specific themes and their development up to the present, even if you find the piece disjointed and disagreeable and even if the opening sections are forgotten, one can still have the continuous and indubitable awareness of listening to the same piece of music. Identity can indeed persist despite a considerable failure to grasp the more particular content of experience. In the case of a concert, one continually has the broad referential frame of the piece beginning, coupled with an awareness that the clapping signaling the end of the piece has not yet taken place. A breakdown of this type of self-identity will occur if the part-whole relation breaks down.

Such a disruption of identity often occurs in dreams, and accounts for much of their strangeness. Consider a case where one is fully cognizant of having a now, but where one does not know what frame of reference the now belongs to, in both its spatial and temporal dimensions (i.e., not knowing the general "where" of the current event, and not knowing its temporal context, such as "my life"). In a dream our identity will still rely on a part-whole relation, but if the whole is not a very great expanse and if it often changes dimensions, then one's identity can become disturbingly volatile and episodic. Amnesia will produce a similar result in waking life. Similarly, a catastrophic event, such as war, may simply destroy the credibility of one's prior life horizon, resulting in a temporary or even a more permanent disruption of identity. Simply waking up in an alien surrounding (e.g., while on holiday) can momentarily unsettle the part-whole gestalt.

Applying these insights to the above notion of life story, we can see that, as for the music example, self-identity may persist in our lives even though particular events and episodes do not mesh together well at all. Such an identity may be grounded on the framing story of life in its most general features, e.g., birth and death as two limits—"they were born, they lived, and they died" is a biography that fits us all. What falls between these two poles becomes part of my life, and that means part of what is considered a unitary phenomenon. This identity, it should be noted, is not the persistence of an entity, a thing (substance, subject, ego), but is a meaning constituted by a relation of figure to ground or part to whole. It is an identity in difference constituted by framing the flux of particular experiences by a broader story.

This continuous, though often implicit, awareness of our identity is an important phenomenon, all we may need in our day-to-day lives, but it requires filling out if our identity is to become more particular and rich. Indeed, we generally know far more of our broad life story than its two limits. It is this still unfolding, developing, even fragmenting story that forms the backdrop of our present. Whereas the birth-death scheme has little content but considerable stability, our particular stories have far greater content but may make little sense to us as a whole. But let us now return to our discussion of the prenarrative.

It should be obvious that there is a dialectic between the prenarrated and the narrated. Narrative is not simply the making public of what already exists in a preexpressed though privately cognized form. What must be stressed, against Mink, is that narrative is a realm of intelligibility that we are already involved in, explicitly and implicitly. But we must not be misled into thinking that the function of a narrative is to report the "facts" of our lives as they were. This sort of simple recounting was disparaged in chapter 1. To narrate experience is, as Ricoeur emphasizes, to refigure it, to tell it in a certain way, and often for a certain end. Self-narration is, as we have previously stressed, both a receptive and a creative-interpretive act. Narration both excludes certain phenomena and dwells on others; it is unavoidably selective. This selectivity is clearly manifested at the level of practical action. Certain acts contribute in a productive way to achieving a goal, while others are abortive. Certain people and events are instrumental to our destiny, while others are not. Again, many of our daily tasks are routine and mundane, performed in a like fashion by numerous other people in their daily lives. Narrative may of course recount these banal daily events, but a story traditionally seeks the exceptional and formative (while perhaps seeking the exemplary and universal).

In considering what prenarrative experience is like we are treading close to what Wilfrid Sellers has called the myth of the given, the myth that there is a realm of experience prior to, and amenable to, expression in language. But we need not go this far. Language, culture, and, as Heidegger has shown, understanding cannot be subtracted from experience without doing violence to our humanity. Our experience is already what we have called a quasi-narrative, a story to be told and one that is partially told already. We need only consider the sophistication of dreams to see just how far narrative is a part of our constitution. Barbara Hardy, in the passage cited earlier, indicates the pervasiveness of narrative emplotment, and at a level that is not explicitly reflective. In other words, we often undergo experience in narrative sequences quite automatically, without choice. These may not be the full-blown narratives of autobiographies or stories, but they can serve in the same way to generate understanding, direction, and unity in our lives.

We tend explicitly to narrate longer temporal sequences only when the situation calls for it. Perhaps a dilemma calls for a reassessment of our project, or a lover asks for our history, or maybe we are in psychotherapy. If we are not always narrating ourselves in order to understand who we are, it is because this second-order reflection is not necessarily required for everyday praxis. We do not, for example, need continually to reformulate or consciously remember our initial rationale or desires to continue meaningfully a present action to its conclusion; this could even be counterproductive. Much of the time our identity is not a concern for us because it is unthematically supported by the regularities in our day-to-day experience: our body, work, friends, home, and general style of living. In addition, our narratives are often no more than verbal tokens, stating, for example, name, address, occupation, and the like. These latter examples are narratives only in a weak sense, for while they are indeed narrated they nevertheless contain no real story or personal history; they do not connect with our prenarrative temporal experience. To be satisfied with such "narratives" is to be satisfied with a shallow sense of one's own existence and personal identity.

Hardy states some further instances of narrative in her list. I have already referred to dreams, and that the same applies to daydreams should be quite clear. To daydream is preeminently to construct a narrative story, one that weaves language and pictorial fantasy together into the forms of our desire. But daydreams can easily pass over into the images of anticipation, hope, hatred, and despair, each of which develops along the beginning-middle-end structure of a narrative. I want to consider emotion in more detail both because of its importance in our lives and because its structure carries over into many of the above areas.

Narrative and Emotion

If human experience indeed has a quasi-narrative nature (prior to our "imposition" of art on life), then we ought to be able to substantiate this claim by discovering in our emotional life a throughgoing and essential narrative ingredient. We shall primarily be appealing to the work of Charles Taylor to support this view. Throughout, we will also be interested in the implications of this position for our sense of self, and especially for our self-understanding.

Much of our emotional life is bound up with the way we narrate experiences (both past and present). It would be difficult, for example, to imagine someone experiencing guilt, joy, or anxiety without having some cognizance of the events to which these emotions are the responses, and beyond this to the story in which the events take on significance. As I have argued, the narration of events is not a simple description of "facts" but an interpretive activity—it is an important way in which our experiences are understood, are given form and meaning. Prior to some degree of narration, the *meaning* of human events for us is obscure or simply absent. This situation is like comparing a chronicle to a full historical narrative; the chronicle merely states occurrences whose further relevance remains to be interpreted. If, therefore, narration is linked to emotions, then emotions are likely to be keyed to, or dependent on, the type of interpretation we give of events in our lives.

Taylor's essay "Self-Interpreting Animals" offers useful insights into the relation between language, narrative, and emotion.[33] Many important feelings or emotions are, he claims, self-referential in that they arise from a certain articulated awareness of one's life situation. As the various imports on this linguistic level of description change, so do the correlative feelings. An inflicted wound, for example, tends to be felt as painful no matter what we think (i.e., is not narratively self-referential), but that this leads to the further and more distinctly human feeling of anxiety, say, or indignation toward one's assailant will very much depend upon one's articulation of the meaning the event has in its broader context; it will also depend on a certain preunderstanding of oneself. These latter, "higher" types of emotion are, Taylor maintains, a product of interpretation and are properly self-referential.

To use an example of Taylor's: if we were unable to experience shame, then "a world without beings capable of this kind of experience would be one without any aspiration to dignity" (SA, p. 53), for the experience of shame is manifest only against the background of leading a life where one desires a certain respect from others. "Thus the import of shameful can be explicated only by reference to a subject who experiences his world in a certain way" (SA, p. 53). Emotions like shame must, therefore, be viewed as an indication of "what is important to us qua subjects . . . , what we value, or what matters to us" (SA, p. 60), even though we may be only partially aware of this background. It is because of this self-referential element, this reference to the broader life of the subject, that such higher emotions, says Taylor, "do not fit into an objectivist's view of the world" (SA, p. 55). If this claim is true, then at least some emotions cannot be reduced to bodily states that the predelineated subject simply endures, but are, on a narrative account, part and parcel of what it means to be a subject.

To see the central place of narrative in emotional experience we must pursue Taylor's analysis a little further. The types of emotion he is concerned with all involve some degree of interpretive articulation, which, because of the reflexivity to the subject's life, is also a form of self-understanding. In brief, such emotions are language dependent: "To say that language is constitutive of emotion is to say that experiencing an emotion essentially involves seeing that certain descriptions apply" (SA, p. 71).[34] What this implies is that the emotion is concomitant with an articulated judgment concerning a given state of affairs. One sees, via something like Santayana's moral imagination, that a situation is "bad" or "degrading" and one experiences therefore the attendant affect. The important point to be noted here is that the initial insight into the context or implicit story is inseparably bound up with the resultant emotion.

Emotions also have a life history, for they change during the course of our developing understanding:

> The remorse may dissipate altogether, if we come to see that our sense of wrong-doing is unfounded; or it may alter in other ways, as we come to

understand what is wrong; perhaps it will be more acute as we see how grave the offence was; perhaps it will be less as we see how hard it was to avoid. (SA, p. 63)

This account is reminiscent of our earlier discussion of the relation between the prenarrative drama and the explicit narrative level. Very often the "truth" of one does not carry over into the other, and we must continually adjust our story until we are satisfied that "this is how it was." Experienced satisfaction and a sense of adequacy are major arbiters here, though they should not be assimilated to a naive representational theory.

Emotional experiences are, however, not only the result of interpretive emplotment but also the occasion for it. In promoting interpretation, emotions "open us to the domain of what it is to be human" (SA, p. 64). Language, in articulating the import of emotions, discloses what is important to us in our lives (what we get upset, angry, or excited about, and so on) and will serve to define our own character, our values, and our relationship to others. But it should be remembered that this articulation may in turn, as we saw above, change the emotion itself.

Taylor concludes by considering our experience of inarticulate emotion, for this would seem to be a case where the language paradigm falters. He puts the question as follows: "We might be tempted to think of animals as experiencing inarticulately what we give names to" (SA, p. 74). But such inarticulate emotions, Taylor claims, are already *unterwegs zur Sprache* by their very nature, for what characterizes such experiences is precisely their demand for interpretation: "We experience our pre-articulate emotion as perplexing, as raising a question. And this is an experience that no non-language animal can have" (SA, p. 74). Taylor's reason for this demand follows from a position parallel to Heidegger's emphasis on the ontological primacy of both language and understanding. Says Taylor:

Because as language-animals we are already involved in understanding it [emotion/feeling]; we already have incorporated into our language an interpretation of what is really important. And it is this articulation . . . which makes our inarticulate feelings into questions. (SA, p. 74)

Understanding is, we can say, a natural goal in the development of our inarticulate feelings, much as the inchoate episodes of our life, as we saw from Ricoeur, seem to demand narrative emplotment for their understanding and development.

Subject-referring emotions always occur within a social matrix of goals and aspirations, aspirations that naturally achieve clarity and definition in language and often at the instigation of prior emotions that reveal value directions in our lives. Emotions can thereby bring us to ourselves in their demand for understanding; they very often demand a narrative to be unfolded which gives meaning to their manifestation and, thereby, an interpretation to our lives. But it is an already more or less explicit narrative understanding that promulgates our higher-level affective responses from the very start. We have already seen a foundation for this understanding in the prenarrative character of lived experience. Taylor's "we already have incorporated into our language an interpretation of what is really important" specifically points to the extraindividual narratives-beliefs-ideologies that form the very core of any society.

It should be readily apparent that Taylor's account of emotion is directly applicable to a discussion of, say, hope and despair, and can even be carried over to certain forms of doubt and belief (speaking again on the level of self-referential states). All such states make sense only against a background emplotment, against a drama one is cognizant of. One *hopes* for a possible future, one that is already imaginatively delineated, whereas a situation that is *hopeless* is one where an expected or wished-for drama is not being realized, not coming to fruition. In each case one's hopes and aspirations are already linguistically and imagistically mediated in a narrative fashion, and may involve the call to a further understanding, to further development.

Another way of stating that such states are self-referential is to say, borrowing from Gabriel Marcel, that they reflect something we *are* and not merely something we *have.* Our body, as Marcel has shown, functions ambiguously in both of these modes, depending on the perspective we adopt toward it. For example, we may be in pain owing to an accident, but we do not regard the pain as disclosing in some way our personal identity, our selves; it is simply something fairly impersonal we have or are forced to undergo. On the other hand, we consider the higher emotions as disclosive of our natures as individual, goal-directed social begins (for example, in the specific way we deal with pain).

These self-referential states are important because, to quote Taylor, "they ascribe a form to what matters to us" (SA, p. 64). In other words, such states point to or embody important value directions, and in this respect they have moral relevance, especially as our affective states usually relate to the acts of other persons as well as to ourselves. Emotional states must therefore be considered as evaluative, and we have a long tradition that links one's moral leanings to what is particularly characteristic of the human individual.

Taylor sums up his essay:

> Human emotion is interpreted emotion, which is nevertheless seeking its adequate form. This is what is involved in seeing man as a self-interpreting animal. It means that he cannot be understood simply as an object among objects, for his life incorporates an interpretation, an expression of which

> cannot exist unexpressed, because *the self that is to be interpreted is essentially that of a being who self-interprets.* (SA, p. 75, my emphasis)

The human subject, as the existentialists have long maintained, is an unfinished subject. But perhaps more than this it is a subject that continually writes, develops, and often erases its own definition, its story. What lies behind our self-conceptions is not some identical thing-in-itself (soul, self, spirit, ego, etc., though these can have a place within a narratological theory), but rather language as it derives from our sedimented history, especially the autobiographical language of self-narration. If I am a being who self-interprets, then it is to the interpreting itself that we should turn; we should not think that we can escape this circularity by recourse to a self external or transcendent to this act.

I am not saying, nor is Taylor, that consciousness equals language. It is rather the case that the various orders of human reality are invariably cut through with language and that the diversity and depth of experienced meaning in our lives is preeminently a result of our linguistic and storytelling nature, or at least has articulation and conceptual understanding as a goal.[35] Much of this experienced meaning, however, derives from our linguistic-cultural heritage and may remain in the background in ordinary praxis—just as our developing life story may remain horizonal. A self-interpreting animal is one that can define itself anew, that can discard or embellish its old definitions. As self-interpreters we therefore have responsibility for our selves, for the selves we were and the selves we would wish to become.

Before we examine the status of the narrating subject in more detail, it will be instructive to conclude this chapter on narrative by considering an important area that has been only a side issue in my preceding account: the relation between narrative and morality. It should be clear, especially from literature, that stories (fictional or otherwise) do not recount a mere string of details that have no human interest; nor do they describe events in an objective or neutral fashion (no matter what the author's avowed intention may be). Narratives grow out of a social milieu and cannot help but reflect and augment (positively or negatively) its values and concerns. We shall also see that one's personal narrative is woven into a social structure, and is not fully of one's own making.

The Virtue of Narrative

Each human life traces out a complex figure that necessarily intersects and interacts with the figures of others.[36] Social action therefore immediately involves us in various plots and subplots, many of which we are only passively entangled in. We have already outlined the prenarrative quality of experience, and there is more to be said about it. This social matrix of plots is the material, or subtext, out of which our more explicit self-reflections are formed along their narrative threads, both retrospectively and prospectively. In this respect, we might say that narration is a secondary process,[37] that of a story becoming known, becoming explicit. But although narration is a secondary process, it is an essential one with respect to human understanding because it places acts in relation to each other and discloses those *Gestalten* and continuities without which understanding would prove infertile.

To narrate the figure of the past is, in addition, to attempt a retrieval of ourselves on the plane of self-understanding. It is to create a portrait of ourselves, no matter how badly delineated. Without this recuperative act there would be little or no content to the "I" that I am for myself; there would not be the reflection that is so characteristic of human agents. As Taylor has written, "there is no such thing as what [human beings] are, independently of how they understand themselves."[38] It is a question of what, in reflection, we make of our situation vis-à-vis the past, present, and future. Our conceptions (disclosed in stories) may even reveal a multiplicity of selves; this is a phenomenon more common than is often suspected, and one I shall say more about later.

Self-portrayal is a form of what might be called representation, where this does not imply a mirroring of the past but rather a generation of something that *stands for* the past (or myself in the past); what I previously called a *representative*. The mirroring relation is not, however, totally alien to our experience, for our tellings are very often retellings, where one story may or may not reflect or correspond to another from a prior date (or to another person's account). In this respect there is often considerable intertextuality in our remembering—the tale is retold, and relates to little but a prior telling. In fact, much of what we remember is simply a prior remembering, a prior emplotment.

There are many reasons why experience gets narrated or represented, some of which I have alluded to in earlier sections, but in the realm of social action this is primarily because, as Ricoeur remarks, "human lives need and merit being narrated."[39] The "need" is manyfold and ties in not only with constituting our identity (as an individual, as a nation, etc.), but also with justifying our very existence, our acts (Sartre's *Nausea,* for example, concludes on this note). This form of narrating is a sort of moral imperative.

Narratives also reveal aspects or "truths" of our life that would otherwise remain obscure or simply unconstituted. Human lives "merit" narration not only because they can be exemplary and heroic but also because they should not be forgotten: "The whole history of suffering cries out for vengeance and calls for narrative," claims Ricoeur.[40] In this respect one need only remember the holocaust and the literature it gave rise to, or rather demanded (the poetry of Nelly Sachs and Paul Celan, for example).

Finally, we might also add to this list of reasons for narration that human lives are quite simply intrinsically interesting.

Human action is valorized action, if only because it involves choice and deliberation, and it is narration that carries over to explicit consciousness action's implicit moral tenor and attempts to preserve it. This is, of course, a virtue of novels and biographies over philosophical discourse. It is especially in novels that we discover a whole gamut of possible moral values and positions, a great number of which we might not otherwise come upon and understand. Without narration the past would sink into an obscurity of forgetfulness wherein everything becomes equal. Narrative, however, not only delivers over the past but is also the medium of our aspirations and desires, imaginatively expressing, in the stories we tell ourselves and those others that we hear and read, a possible future with its attendant joys and hardships and, hence, possible selves.

The stories we tell are part and parcel of our becoming. They are a mode of vision, plotting what is good and what is bad for us, what is possible and what is not—plotting who we may become. But in the telling we seem also to be immediately involved in generating the *value* of a certain state of affairs or course of action, of judging its worth, ethical or otherwise. We have already explained how recollection does not simply describe but tends also to dramatize human events, and in so doing it places them in hierarchical relations to each other, even if this only amounts to raising certain material to momentary prominence. In the sphere of social action this valorization understandably takes the form of moral judgment and critique, contributing thereby to the ethical realm of our existence. This ethical aspect of narration, taken somewhat broadly, is what I now wish to consider.

It was a general thesis of George Santayana that neither perception nor experience can be reperceived or remembered; they can only be imaginatively reconstructed, dramatized in images and words. He gives the name "literary psychology" to this sphere: "Scientific psychology is a part of physics, or of the study of nature; it is the record of how animals act. Literary psychology is the art of imagining how they think and feel." Scientific psychology, as Santayana defined it, addresses the animate world in terms of observable (at least theoretically) material events, whereas literary psychology addresses these same events as they are "transposed into the broad realm of experienced significance on the part of conscious human subjects." This significance needs to be apprehended, says Santayana, "dramatically, by imitative sympathy," where it is especially this intersubjective sympathetic element that escapes the purview of an objective science: "literary psychology, however far scientific psychology may push it back, always remains in possession of the moral field."[41] Such moral values, as we shall see, are very much a product of how experience is reconstituted and sustained in our narrative reflections. We have already had occasion to mention, in this respect, Santayana's important notion of the "moral imagination."

What follows from the above brief account is that values are very much indigenous to the story, to the way in which events are related, and can only be abstracted from this context secondarily. In the same way that emotions generally vary with our articulated understanding of events (and vice versa), so does the value attending those events. It would not be pertinent to our topic of narrative to enter into a detailed discussion of the relation between emotion and value, but it should be clear that in experience we cannot really separate emotion and value; together they contribute to the meaning or significance our life has in most, if not all, of its less mundane episodes. What "literary psychology" and "moral imagination" seek to display in their narrative reconstructions is precisely this significance, and it is an endeavor closely paralleled by the novelist's enterprise.

A primary difference between literature and the world of concrete action is of course that the significance of the latter often demands immediate physical action from us (we must respond, say, with more than just understanding and compassion), and this reaction may bring about further responses (tied to our concrete involvement and ability to act), though not always. Many events that we hear of and many that we witness do not demand our practical intervention, and in this respect they may closely resemble our response to what we may read. The text or plots of life may result in much the same responses as do literary texts, and this is especially true on the level of valuation. This is why art can imitate life and vice versa, with advantages gained by both. In life and art, narrative and significance work in a symbiotic relationship. For example, the story (or memory) may call forth the emotional response. Likewise, the emotion may call forth the story (or the memory). Thus writers will often let the unfolding plot determine the emotional-valuational result, but they may also guide the plot in light of a response they wish to attain, a value they wish to exemplify. Either way, in life as in art there is an interweaving of narrative and significance (value).

Values arise in the drama of our life, especially in the choices this life involves. It should be understandable, then, why dramatization is the form of expression most adequate to the direct disclosure of human action in its social and moral significance, and hence for disclosing individuals in their characteristic (and valorized) traits and identities: as villainous, heroic, vain, humble, and so on. In the relating of actual human lives, dramatization must of course occur after the fact. As Arendt has written, the "unchangeable identity of a person, though disclosing itself intangibly in act and speech, becomes tangible only in the story of the actor's and speaker's life."[42] One is reminded here of Ulysses narrating his own past endeavors and trials to the Phaiakeans.

There appears to be some truth in saying, as Max Scheler did, that "the whole person is contained in every fully concrete act."[43] But it is true only for someone who can then interpret those acts into meaningful sequences, someone who can "see" or imagine the broader story. For as we have seen, the significance of human action is understood in and through the reflection that the acts give rise to, from the context or framing story in which they fit. It is not that the self is behind the acts, visible and fully formed at their inception; the self is rather a result of actions, something that actions imply.

Again we are back at the implicit story that is waiting, as it were, to be told, to be revealed, and that on being revealed will disclose the implied subject of the actions (the actor) in his or her valorized dimensions. This revelation is, as we have seen, always interpretive, not the neutral description of a prior and nonlinguistic objectivity. Another way of saying this is that the self is a "reference" produced via the interpretation, projected by it. Ricoeur uses a similar notion when he talks of the world set up by a literary text as its "productive reference"—allowing him to circumvent naive objectivism.[44]

Given that the self belongs in a teleological (though perhaps fairly short-range) and storylike framework, it seems necessary that one's life exhibit something like a unity of purpose if it is not to be fragmented (or multiple) and unstable. It is on this level of purposes and intentions that our characteristic human identity, personal identity, is especially evident, for it is here that value determinations relating to the form of life that we lead are disclosed; as Taylor contends, "our identity is defined by our fundamental evaluations."[45] Telling a person's story tends invariably to plot the type of moral agent he or she is or was; it reveals the value directions in his or her life by selectively plotting only those actions relevant or tributary to certain central purposes.

In the same way that a story traditionally demands followability and closure, we tend to expect unity and continuity in other people's lives and in our own. No matter how disorganized and disjunct a life may appear, the biographer's art, like reflection generally, has always been to "reduce" diversity to a perhaps hidden unity, a purpose, central disposition, or group of problems that even the actor may not have been aware of. Sartre's existential psychoanalysis, for example, makes this point (while, however, contradicting some of his other more relativistic claims!). A story that does not provide us with such a unity is usually regarded as a failed or incomplete story. A life may similarly be considered incomplete; it is a life that does not facilitate some degree of final understanding and judgment. Although there are some obvious problems with this traditional position aimed at unity and closure, it nevertheless still affords insight into the function of narrative in this area.

In our own lives, and in our own self-understanding, the achievement of unity is usually considered necessary for our identity; and in our social life, unity of purpose and consistency of valuation form part of what it means to be a responsible moral agent. Responsibility accrues to a person who can evaluate possible acts with respect to their worth, as noble or base, as cowardly or courageous, and so on. In this realm one cannot help but appeal to an *already* constituted vocabulary of personal values. An extreme existentialist position of radical choice would make no sense precisely because one must there eschew such "traditional" values (as a basis for choosing) and seemingly, therefore, evaluate out of thin air. Evaluation, however, is impossible in such a vacuum. Autonomy does not mean the complete overthrow of the past; it implies, rather, that possible actions are evaluated in light of the values I *already* accept responsibility for, values that are already determinants for the direction of my life and therefore for the type of person that I am. As Taylor writes, "Moral agency . . . requires some kind of reflexive awareness of the standards one is living by"[46] (or failing to live by). It is the latter horizon of values that allows further evaluations to be made.

If we now look in more detail at the evaluation procedure, we find, as with the higher emotions, that it is significantly mediated through language, particularly the language of a learned vocabulary of contrasting values. On this question we shall primarily follow Taylor's analysis.[47] Taylor's principal claim is that evaluation is of two fairly distinct types, weak and strong, and that only the latter properly reflects a self-formation of the subject and hence a formation of the type of life the subject leads. Weak evaluation is a judgment that simply considers outcomes and operates on the principle of greater or less desirability. What is lacking here, from the point of view of strong evaluation, is a qualitative judgment concerning the relative worth of such desires. Weak evaluation, in the extreme case, does not enter upon the path of rejecting a desirable alternative because it is, say, base or cowardly; such considerations of worth arise only with a higher or second level reflection:

> In weak evaluation, for something to be judged good it is sufficient that it be desired, whereas in strong evaluation there is also a use of "good" or some other evaluative term for which being desired is not sufficient. . . . (*Agency*, p. 18)

In this way I may set up second-order desires which situate me in the properly human realm of morals and values; only at this point am I significantly different from other animal species (*Agency*, pp. 15ff).

In our consideration of emotions we noted that whereas lower-level feelings, such as pain and bodily disturbances generally, are simply given (or can be so considered for our purposes), the self-referential emotions are a product of how we articulate or plot a given state of affairs. This same structure, if I follow Taylor correctly, applies to evaluation. The truly ethical realm is not a pregiven stratum of experience, with attendant objective values that it is our job to discern and our duty to follow, but is again tied into our articulation of a given existential situation or proposed action. The situation prompts our evaluation and our evaluation reflects, dialectically, back onto the situation and valorizes it.

Sartre is thus correct in insisting that we create values and that we define ourselves in and through this creative process; that is, as someone who upholds a particular value or set of values. That we so define ourselves is manifest precisely in the responsibility we feel for our decisions (and I am only talking here about authentic choices, not of cases where one blindly follows custom), and also therefore for the guilt we may well experience. Sartre's account of "bad faith" is again instructive here. Guilt is especially notable for bringing us, via its insistence on being interpreted, to a strong sense of our own being, our own deep-seated values. Guilt, like the inarticulate feelings I earlier discussed, seems to demand a narrative working out of itself.

Such values, or value dispositions, are at once the foundation for my estimations of worth and the habitual basis of myself as a responsible social agent. They are evidenced not only in my acts but also in the stories that I weave to justify such acts. These abiding values are always disclosed to some degree in our present evaluations. This is why our strong evaluations are self-referential (and referential to society) and also self-constitutive. The latter point is important because (a) strong evaluations imply a degree of self-emplotment and (b) many of our evaluations do not simply reflect pregiven dispositions (or expectations) but may go beyond them, perhaps to enhance and deepen them. We may, for example, surprise ourselves in our own estimations and judgments—just as we may in our stories and dreams. To draw a textual (and hermeneutic) analogy, it is from our fund of knowledge about the world and about language that we are able to constitute and appreciate the intricate plot of a novel. But the novel, in turn, may not leave us as innocent as before we read it. In the end the novel speaks about us.

Present evaluations and judgments are thus founded on our cultural past, both our personal past and the broader historical horizon that delimits the possibilities for our mode of life. We are, as MacIntyre claims, "bearers of tradition,"[48] and it is what we inherit from this tradition that forms and continues to guide our initial moral perspectives. As social beings we are already caught up in a network of expectations and obligations, and hence of values that we either sustain or attempt to defuse. Such values are embodied in the practices of a society (as they are in the practices of individuals), and are made public and legitimized in the narratives surrounding them. Thus we have the practice of scientific research, ostensibly motivated by the search for truth, and the further story that legitimizes this research by appealing, say, to a pragmatic telos—future benefit to the quality of human life and such like. Here narrative, revealing its kinship with rhetoric, is a medium of justification as well as of persuasion.

Narrative, then, articulates what is of value to us and why, for it essentially defines (in the first instance) who we are and what we want—in cosmologies, eschatologies, histories, etc. It is a moralizing force that embodies and exemplifies the norms (customs) by which people gain identity and that provides criteria of judgment for acts that occur within the society it defines. This social force of narratives (myths, fables, legends, etc.) is perhaps more immediately discernible in "primitive" societies than in our vast and diversified Western culture, though the real reason for this may well be not a lack of narratives but simply our embeddedness in them and the myopia this lack of distance often leads to.

The above analysis of key themes in Taylor's work sought to show its relevance within the broader framework of a narrative theory of selfhood. In this regard, it is interesting to note that Taylor's recent book, *Sources of the Self,* makes this connection far more explicit.[49] This rich work is at once an account of our present moral situation and a consideration of the notion of selfhood this situation implies. There are, claims Taylor, deep-seated values that operate on an intuitive level in our more important moral evaluations. Such values (e.g., respect for others, freedom, and dignity) can be found to underlie our modern culture, but they require explicit articulation if we are to extricate ourselves from the more superficial and fragmentary world views we consciously operate with and within. Taylor's work, then, aims at articulating the genesis or history of this modern identity and its associated values.

On the personal level this identity, as in his earlier work, is tied to our sense of what is morally good: "My identity is defined by the commitments and identifications which provide the frame or horizon within which I can try to determine from case to case what is good, or valuable, or what ought to be done, or what I endorse or oppose."[50] To lack such a framework is, for Taylor, to exist in something approaching a pathological condition. To define myself is thus to become conversant with the values I operate by and am oriented toward in my ongoing actions and choices. Attaining this understanding is necessarily an interpretative or hermeneutic endeavor involving both our situatedness in language and the sense of our lives as an ongoing project or developing story: "we see that the sense of the good has to be woven into my understanding of my life as an unfolding story. But this is to state another basic condition of making sense of ourselves, that we grasp our lives in a *narrative*."[51] Only narrative, Taylor maintains, can offer a coherent answer to the persistent questions concerning our identity.

How Taylor's account of selfhood differs from many traditional theories of the self (from Descartes to Parfit) is precisely in his emphasis on the cardinal importance of moral values to self-identity.[52] Values that have a central significance for persons and how they live their lives must be considered a key factor in the identity of such persons. The crucial role here of narrative is, ideally, to articulate our life as an organic whole (as for MacIntyre) and disclose thereby the various purposes, and hence values, that both guide and define us as engaged human agents. The crisis of our modern identity is thus, for Taylor, intimately linked to both the loss of a unifying framework or grand narrative (rooted in stable, even universal, values and commitments) through which we make sense of our lives and, concomitant with this, the inability to see our lives as an evolving temporal whole and on the model of a quest. It is unclear, however, if in the last resort Taylor allows for the effect of a continual interdependency or folding back of narratives onto values.

Charles Taylor and, before him, Alasdair MacIntyre are of course not the only contemporary thinkers in North America who have emphasized the importance of narrative for ethical theory; the work of Stanley Hauerwas is also important in this regard. An insightful paper by Hauerwas and David Burrell poses interesting points concerning the question of narrative versus rationality in ethics.[53] The problem they raise concerns the disparagement of narrative understanding (and narrative rationality) in face of a more disengaged and traditional notion of rational appraisal of ethical matters: "contemporary ethical theory has tried to secure for moral judgments an objectivity that would free such judgments from subjective beliefs, wants, and stories of the agents who make them" (HB, p. 16). The model here is the prevalent and influential scientific method of impersonal and instrumental rationality that aims to free practice "from the arbitrary and contingent nature of the agent's beliefs, dispositions, and character" (HB, p. 16).

In contradistinction to this "scientific" approach, Hauerwas and Burrell make these claims:

> (1) that character and moral notions only take on meaning in a narrative; (2) that narrative and explanation stand in an intimate relationship, and, therefore, moral disagreements involve rival histories of explanation; (3) that the standard account of moral objectivity is the obverse of existential ethics, since the latter assumes that the failure to secure moral objectivity implies that all moral judgments must be subjective or arbitrary. (HB, p. 15)

The first point we have already explored to quite a degree. It is a claim that squarely situates morality and moral notions in the ongoing storied life of human agents. It also stresses that moral notions are tied to the character of individuals and to the moral improvement of character. It is not enough to say that one ought to be good, for we also require insight into what the good might be. In other words, we require stories that exemplify the good as put into practice, stories that teach us "to know and do what is right under definite conditions" (HB, p. 16).

The second point gets at the heart of moral disagreements by indicating the important explanatory power of narrative. Another way of putting this is to say, as we mentioned earlier, that narrative legitimizes practice; it is explanatory, but in a way different from a rationality that seeks impersonal grounding principles from which to explain deductively the nature of morality. A narrative position accepts the embeddedness of moral practices in a variety of traditions that in turn support a rich variety of beliefs and dispositions.

The third point is intended to steer a course between objectivism and subjectivism, both being seen as false options. Against objectivism the claim is made that we should turn to the life situations of moral subjects and to their own narrative interpretations of their conduct. Against subjectivism Hauerwas and Burrell contend that this position does not get one into a relativistic individualism:

> The fact is that the first person singular is seldom the assertion of the solitary "I". . . . For our experiences always come in the form of narratives that can be checked against themselves as well as others' experiences. I cannot make my behavior mean anything I want it to mean, for I have learned from others. The language the agent uses to describe his behavior, to himself and to others, is not uniquely his—it is *ours*. (HB, p. 21)

Objectivism would separate moral principles from ongoing life or place them in a hypothetical realm preceding the formation of a particular culture (e.g., categorical imperatives and various contractarian approaches), while subjectivism would ignore the sedimented and shared values of the traditions which serve to define our very world view, whether we are conscious of this determination or not.

Hauerwas's and Burrell's quarrel with rationalism has much to do with its presupposed freedom from particular practices and times, as though it were a transcendental judge of human affairs. But, they contend, this is not the case: "All our notions are narrative-dependent, including the notion of rationality" (HB, p. 21). Here we are closer to a view of rationality as rhetoric, and therefore as guided by current interests and purposes. In arguing for or against abortion, for example, we usually cannot help but invoke and work out of a narrative context that defines the role of, say, children, procreation, and motherhood in our lives (HB, p. 22).

Our moral notions are intimately tied to such narratives, and we hold such notions because of the value they have for our character and, more generally, "for directing our life-projects and shaping our stories" (HB, p. 22). But narratively embedded moral notions need not, of course, be considered irrational. A good story always has a high degree of rational intelligibility, though it is not the rationality of a scientific exposition that plots linear and *necessary* connections between phenomena.

Discriminating among stories, say Hauerwas and Burrell, "is less a matter of weighing arguments than of displaying how adopting different stories will lead us to become different sorts of persons" (HB, p. 35). For in the end it is the formation of character (along with its important social dimension) that is crucial in moral considerations. Not "on what principles should we base our actions?" and not simply "how should we behave?" but also "how should we behave in order to become better persons?"—where persons are known only in a historico-narrative context.

Hauerwas and Burrell offer criteria for judging the possible effects of stories, including the "power to release us from destructive alternatives," "seeing through current distortions," and "room to keep us from having to resort to violence" (HB, p. 35). Narrative literature (e.g., biblical stories, novels, poetry) clearly serves as an organ for the investigation and representation of various life practices and pursuits, plotting possible outcomes for the characters, along with their associated values. They thereby allow us to experience and judge the value of life-styles and ideologies at a distance, without having to undergo the experience firsthand in our own lives. We learn, for example, tolerance of alternate life-styles. We learn the negative value and workings of deception and deceit. We are exposed to the ideologies that can lead only to mental or physical destruction. In sum, we are exposed, perhaps for the first time, to the whole gamut of human social values, an exposure that tends invariably to develop and sharpen our moral perception and interpretations and serve to give form to our actions in a way that instrumental rationalism either overlooks or grossly understates.

In Paul Ricoeur's terms, the worlds that are opened up by narratives offer new possibilities to the reading or listening subject; they are worlds that both involve and affect the subject. In the end such experiences may lead to an active refiguration of the subject's own world and practices, giving them new significance and previously unseen purposes—which is, in effect, to change the character of the subject.[54]

It is a commonplace that our age has often been characterized as lacking a guiding telos, a modern mythology in light of which we can view ourselves, gain identity, and have clearly defined purposes, though science and technology do perform this task to some degree, usurping religion (among other things) in the process. Jean-François Lyotard characterizes our age as not only lacking a "meta-narrative," a single story uniting human endeavor and aspirations to a single goal, but also as being distrustful of such a thing.[55] In his praise of multiplicity and segmentation Lyotard goes as far as seeing the virtue of promoting a schizophrenic, divided identity (this is both descriptive and normative for Lyotard).

The power of totalizing ideologies is of course Lyotard's primary target, but from our point of view the sheer stress on the pervasive influence of narrative is informative. Narratives, and especially meta-narratives, are part of the very fabric of culture and tradition. This phenomenon is clear in small tribal communities where the whole social structure, and the subjects within it, may be guided and regulated by what we call a mythological world view. Once under the sway of such narratives life becomes simply a repetition of the same stages and orders that are there represented, from the broader social structure down to the individual life and its development. In such a world view virtue is tantamount to fulfilling an expected role in society; one performs well or ill what tradition demands, and there may be very little leeway or toleration for deviation.

Narratives are clearly a primary vehicle of ideologies, both nationally and on the level of the individual—the ideologies we inherit and those we fabricate in our conversations with ourselves and others—and they are a powerful force in providing a delimited world where good is good and bad is bad. But we are aware of what happens to many of the values we upheld in earlier days; things quite simply tend toward change. A critical reflection is necessary if our stories, our self-conceptions and possibilities, are not to become confining or stagnant, and if they are to keep in touch with the prenarrative level. Traditions, like individuals, should allow for conflict and variation if they are to remain healthy and not decline.[56]

Narratives, traditionally conceived, seem inherently moralizing. The closure to human actions that they effect is often that of promoting one moral order over another. This is a thesis of Hayden White, one that he finds active in historical texts: "it seems possible to conclude that every historical narrative has as its latent or manifest purpose the desire to moralize the events of which it treats."[57] As such, a narrative is a moral drama that serves in the last resort as an interpretation and judgment of the events related, especially with a view to offering an overview of, while deciding between, conflicting interpretations. A prime example of such conflict is that which guided much of Hegel's thinking in this area—Sophocles' *Antigone*—where we find played out the conflict of divine law versus the king's law. This situation is similarly reflected in the more prevalent conflict between personal desire and law. Much of our own narrating can usefully be seen as driven by some such conflict, tension, or crisis in our own lives.[58]

It is a commonly accepted view that a stringent and unswerving self-conception is a sign of possible intolerance toward people with a different outlook. One totalizes one's own position, one's own account (or belief) of what the good life consists in, and becomes blind to alternatives. This blindness spreads to the understanding of other positions, which are simply discarded rather than understood. This situation especially applies to the dogmatist, who perhaps lacks both imagination and a certain playfulness and has ears only for that which he already believes. Our previous discussion points both to the value and the potential danger of such closure. But closure is often belied by the actual subtext of action (the prenarrative level); a subtext exhibiting divergences and contradictions that are not taken up in the explicit narrative enterprise. Self-understanding rides tandem with an encountering of otherness, with an imaginative empathy for the other that in turn discloses or develops possibilities for oneself. How, indeed, can one understand that which is not a *possibility* for oneself or that which one has already closed off?

The individual is in fact something of a chameleon, adapting itself very much to the needs of the moment. The structures that support our existence are not static like the frame of a building or automobile. In mankind these structures are especially flexible and adaptive, able to accommodate the new and to give birth to it (the "structuring structures" of Bourdieu). Structure is aimed at performance, at work. In other words, one's habitus is what gears into the present praxial situation, transforming the world. Viewed in this way, structure alone, and not the superficial exploits of some supposed ego, is a force for creativity. This is, incidentally, why creativity is not easily taught and why it effects its best work passively rather than in accordance with the demands of a thinking-willing subject.

Identity rides on a more or less continuous history of difference, identified and unified more by a route, a history, than by an essence (consider the diverse route of Augustine). The center of my identity is preeminently the present itself and my certainty that I am this present, that it is me (the speaking-thinking subject). Yet in this present I change. I relocate myself or, more precisely, reword myself. I was "there," now I am "here". I was "that," now I am "this."[59] Language in this way situates the subject within a chorus of temporal and spatial shifters; language opens a past and a future where the subject is caught in its own signifying practice, sustained by it, produced by it. As Emile Benveniste discovered, "Language is . . . the possibility of subjectivity because it always contains the linguistic forms appropriate to the expression of subjectivity. . . ."[60] In language (and in expression generally) "I" am set free; but do "I" really speak? With Michel Foucault I maintain that the performing self, the self as origin and originator, is in certain important respects an unnecessary hypothesis.[61] Given what we have so far seen of the self, the question is what role or position does the subject now have, now that it is displaced from center field?

Having shown the relevance of narrative to our lives generally—its role in personal identity, understanding, emotions, values, and cultural identity—we shall now pursue in more detail the question of the individual's relation to language and to his or her own story. This investigation will yield systematization of the self in terms of a play of semiotic positions–of speaking, spoken, and implied subjects.

III

THE SUBJECT

Language reproduces the world, but by submitting it to its own organization.

Emile Benveniste
Problems in General Linguistics

Man speaks, then, but it is because the symbol has made him man.

Jacques Lacan
Ecrits: A Selection

In chapter 1, I maintained that the human subject cannot be considered, in terms of temporality or memory, without a considerable intervention of narrational activity. Chapter 2 built on this earlier work by sketching the significance of narrative for a number of more specific, but important, aspects of concrete human experience. It is now time to zero in much more specifically on how the self is actually generated and sustained by expressive acts. Of particular importance will be the function and meaning of that little but highly important pronoun *I* and the cogito it is implied by.

Many of our mistaken or confused beliefs about the self and our identity result from a naive or misguided conception of language and of the role language plays in our lives. Accordingly, we will begin by looking at three of these interrelated misconceptions; they were more or less explicitly addressed throughout earlier chapters.

It has already been noted that language tempts us to posit, as Nietzsche said, a "doer before the deed"—an "I" that thinks, an "I" that acts. I have argued, however, that the "I" is an implicate of these practices rather than a cause of them. Tied to this problem is a second: the belief in intentions or "thoughts" that exist prior to their linguistic expression. Everyday discourse leads us to suppose that language is a medium for the communication of such thoughts, that it gives voice to them, makes them public. Here language is once removed from the more originary thought or, as it is often called, the authorial intention. Ideally, it is maintained, language neutrally mirrors, reflects, or re-presents this thought, makes it present again in a new medium.

Which brings us to the third misconception: that language has a certain neutrality or transparency with respect to what is expressed, with respect to "reality." Language is a neutral vehicle which is secondary to the message conveyed and is therefore simply overlooked. This leads us, in an especially metaphysical movement, to sever our categories of reality from the categories of our particular language and, in effect, from our historicality.[1] This last misconception need not, however, lead us to separate language and reality (making of the latter an unknowable *Ding an sich*), for it is rather the case that, for us, they belong together. The only reality that exists independently of us is precisely one that is not for us other than as posited by us, such as the subatomic model employed by science. World, self, and language belong inseparably together, and develop together.

Language, far from being a mere communication medium, establishes a complex realm of signifying relations that raise up the sensorially given to the level of meaning. To use language is basically to utilize a system of signs which relate one thing or attribute to another in diverse ways, a system in which "I" am—and this is very important—to the degree that I in fact utilize this code, become *signified* in it. This inextricable implication of the subject in language usage is what this chapter seeks to establish.

Whereas—and I am following Emile Benveniste's *Problems in General Linguistics* here—animals are responsive to natural signals which have a direct correlation to physical events (and can be trained to respond to new ones), man uses symbols that may have no natural relation to these events (PGL, p. 24). Symbols, and especially language, have left their roots in natural phenomena behind. Writes Benveniste: "Man invents and understands symbols; the animal does not. . . . Between the sensory-motor function and the representative function is a threshold which only human beings have been able to cross" (PGL, p. 24). One might begin, as a child does, relating to "words," or rather to sounds, as mere signals, precursors of sensory events (e.g., gratification). But later in the child's life the sensory recedes as the signs and more abstract references multiply. One learns, for example, to signify the absent conceptually (a process already prefigured by passive recollection), not only to see but to refer by name to aspects of what is or has been seen. We are thus gradually educated into a broad realm of symbols and signification. But we are also, in this way, educated into the sociocultural sphere.[2]

"Language *reproduces* reality," contends Benveniste, which also means that "reality is produced anew by means of language" (PGL, p. 22). This form of reproduction is in accord with the conceptuality or structuration inherent in the language. It is with language that we grasp reality, and we do so in a manipulatory gesture, the style of which is to a great degree unconscious. Language acts on the world in a manner parallel to the way our silent bodily habitualities make possible our practical life. But although language must be seen as yet another habituality, it has the added dimension of seemingly unlimited reflexivity and expressibility.[3] This reflexive capacity makes all the difference.

Language also "communicates," of course, and in doing so creates a community: "Society is not possible except through language; nor is the individual" (PGL, p. 23). It is in language that my individual perspective on the world is made known, both to others and to myself. Language accordingly allots linguistic functions for this individuality: personal pronouns, particularly *I* and *you*. It is especially in personal pronouns that we reproduce ourselves as individual persons. But this statement must not be misunderstood. By *person* I do not mean just some thing among things, some entity in the world, for persons are, in the words of Charles Taylor, language animals. Thus language is not simply a tool or device used by persons but is part of their very definition. Again we can turn to Benveniste: "It is a speaking man whom we find in the world, a man speaking to another man, and language provides the very definition of man" (PGL, p. 224).[4] The "I" refers neither to a *res extensa* nor to some mysterious *res cogitans* but primarily to a speaker in the act of speaking. This thesis is essentially that of Benveniste,[5] and it will be of value to begin by considering his position in more detail.

He Who Says "Ego"

> I'm in words, made of words, others' words. . . .
>
> Samuel Beckett
> *The Unnamable*

The three misconceptions previously mentioned—the belief in an I that thinks, in thoughts prior to linguistic expression, and in language as a neutral medium of communication—all relate to a construal of the subject in substantial terms, a subject that may indeed come to itself self-reflexively in language but where the core of the self is posited as a prelinguistic datum. This position often relies on a form of consciousness that is directly present to itself, rather like Aristotle's conception of deity (*noesis noeseos*). In opposition to this way of thinking I have sketched a view of self where language takes center stage, especially in the form of narration with its implied subject. As Calvin Schrag has expressed the matter, "The event of self-consciousness is inseparable from the history of saying 'I'."[6] Such a history is primarily that of autobiographical acts, for a meaningful self-consciousness is, as previous chapters have attempted to show, synonymous with self-narration and therefore with self-interpretation. Benveniste sums up this linguistic position:

> It is in and through language that man constitutes himself as a *subject,* because language alone establishes the concept of "ego" in reality, in *its* reality which is that of the being.
>
> The "subjectivity" we are discussing here is the capacity of the speaker to posit himself as "subject." It is defined not by the feeling which everyone experiences of being himself (this feeling, to the degree that it can be taken note of, is only a reflection) but as the psychic unity that transcends the totality of the actual experiences it assembles and that makes the permanence of the consciousness. Now we hold that "subjectivity," whether it is placed in phenomenology or in psychology, as one may wish, is only the emergence in the being of a fundamental property of language. "Ego" is he who *says* "ego." This is where we see the foundation of "subjectivity," which is determined by the linguistic status of "person" (PGL, p. 224).[7]

Subjectivity is attained in discourse by assuming the role of "I" in that discourse. "I" designates this speaking subject at the instance of utterance, just as it designates other speakers in their turn. "'I,'" says Benveniste, "signifies the person who is uttering the present instance of discourse containing 'I'" (PGL, p. 218). But, as Benveniste also reveals, "I" always functions dialogically with an addressee, "you" (singular or plural), and it is here that language guarantees the possibility of sociality and intersubjectivity (PGL, p. 225). One cannot become "I" without an implicit reference to another person, an auditor or narratee—which may be the same subject qua listener. "I" functions in contrast to "you" in much the same way as "here" refers linguistically to "there" rather than to any fixed location. In Lacanian terms, "there" is the other of "here," "you" is the other of "I," and vice versa. Discourse always has its other, which is one way of restating the Saussurean claim that signifiers gain meaning in relation to other signifiers, to a chain of signifiers that is excluded by the utterance but presupposed by it.

"I" has fundamentally a locutionary reality, setting up what I shall call a *subject of speech* (*le sujet de l'énonce*), a form of subject that exists solely in the expression. In the ordinary train of discourse this linguistic subject tends automatically (habitually and implicitly) to be predicated by listeners and readers of its author, which I term the *speaking subject,* which may be the bodily site of the enunciation or the origin of inscription for written language. This form of predication can, I believe, be seen as fundamental for generating what are generally termed "persons" (embodied subjects). But we must not forget that the subject of speech has an important autonomy from its site of production—it may be reproduced in a text or on a tape recorder, and of course it may be purely fictitious.

The main point here is that the subject of speech does not bear a one-to-one relation to the speaking subject, as though the "truth" of the latter is necessarily mirrored in the former. Rather, we should see here a parallel to the dialectical mechanism of prenarrative-narrative that was discussed in the previous chapter. The meaning of the speaking subject (for itself and for others) is only given via its discourse, in which, if not identified with the thematic subject and content of the utterance (as in autobiography), it at least becomes the authorial subject of the utterance. In itself the speaking subject is simply a possible site of utterances, a semiotic body of potential gestures and articulations through which it will make itself known as a particular subject with particular concerns and perspectives on reality. The speaking subject, then, attains selfhood via its expressions—much as the prenarrative attains its expression and fulfilment in a narrative (such as autobiography or history).

Now the obvious rejoinder to this general linguistic position is, once again, that language is, to the contrary, simply more or less adequate to expressing what is prelinguistically already given to us, as individual subjects, in our experience. In other words, I already am prior to expression, and I employ language primarily to communicate with others. But let us look more closely at this prelinguistic realm. Though we undoubtedly have a bodily existence apart from language, I am claiming here that it is in and through language that the dimension of the subject, the self, is generated.

Consider this statement by Helen Keller, who began life as blind, deaf, and mute: "When I learned the meaning of 'I' and 'me' and found that I was something, I began to think. Then consciousness first existed for me." Prior to this self-consciousness, she writes,

> I did not know that I knew aught, or that I lived or acted or desired. I had neither will nor intellect. I was carried along to objects and acts by a certain blind natural impetus. I had a mind which caused me to feel anger, satisfaction, desire. These two facts led those about me to suppose that I willed and thought.

These statements bring out perfectly the effect of language for providing a position and identity for the human subject. Prior to the appropriation of "I," she says, "my mind was in a state of anarchy in which meaningless sensations rioted, and if thought existed, it was so vague and inconsequent, it cannot be made a part of discourse."[8]

If we can trust Keller's description, there simply was no reflective consciousness, no point of view from which future acts are assessed and the past reflected on. Thus there simply was no "I" that she was *for herself.* The only "I," or the only notion of personhood, that existed was the one predicated of her and filled out by others. Yet despite this situation it seems so natural for us native speakers to attribute selfhood, intention, and conscious deliberation to others that we do so to very young children and sometimes even to animals!

Another interesting point arises from Keller's observations. What I have called the prenarrative level of experience seems not to have existed in any organized fashion; instead there is primarily a riot of sensations and impulses which, as Keller aptly put it, "cannot be made a part of discourse." We find confirmation of this state of affairs in the work of Saussure:

> Psychologically our thought—apart from its expression in words—is only a shapeless and indistinct mass. Philosophers and linguists have always agreed in recognizing that without the help of signs we would be unable to make a clear-cut, consistent distinction between two ideas. Without language, thought is a vague, uncharted nebula. There are no pre-existing ideas, and nothing is distinct before the appearance of language.[9]

We thus see that without language, without a modicum of self-narration occurring during the course of one's life, even one's unreflected or preconscious life loses structure, loses some of its implicit narrative.[10] This leads us to the conclusion that if we have not been brought up with stories we cannot expect to find them in our lives, cannot expect to live them.[11] Indeed, the problem here is that the prenarrative and the narrative levels are always intertwined; their histories continually cross and intermix.

Let us be reminded of Benveniste's central tenet, now that it might have a more concrete value:

> it is literally true that the basis of subjectivity is in the exercise of language. . . . there is no other objective testimony to the identity of the subject except that which he himself thus gives about himself." (PGL, p. 226)

We should especially note the implications of this statement. What, for example, are we to do with patients in a catatonic state? Are they still subjects, still persons? On Benveniste's view the question remains open, but borders on the negative. They are generally granted subject status for us only because they once were speaking subjects—we tend to give them the benefit of the doubt. But if self-consciousness is correlative to language, then only a solipsistic interior dialogue can continue to sustain them as subjects, a fact that is most difficult to ascertain.

It is interesting—in films, for example—how even a computer can become a subject (and be treated as one at the discursive level) if it responds with a voice that uses the first-person singular rather than the drone of impersonal information we might otherwise expect. HAL in Stanley Kubrick's *2001* is an obvious example of this subjectifying brought about in speech, and it often occurs without a visible and localizable physical body. Our positive responses to such, usually fictitious, cases can be revealing.

They point, among other things, to a certain acceptable independence of the speaking subject from its concrete state of embodiment—something we encounter regularly with fictional characters in novels.

HAL was successful as a subject because "his" speech respected the dialogical nature of the personal pronouns; he could become "you," the addressee. The "subjectivity" of HAL is different from the subjectifying of animals I mentioned earlier, for here it comes primarily from HAL "himself," not from our own projecting. We are caught up in the dialogic situation his speech engenders; we ourselves are addressed as subjects.[12]

Jacques Lacan has said of communicative interaction that "if I call the person to whom I am speaking by whatever name I choose to give him, I intimate to him the subjective function that he will take on in order to reply to me, even if it is to repudiate this function."[13] It is surprisingly difficult to avoid this "intersubjective" dialogue altogether. Of course, much does depend on the status of the reply, for I may either recognize or refute others as the types of subject they set themselves up to be, or may deny their subjective status completely by simply not responding to the speech situation at all. This latter case, however, may still form two categories: (1) relegating the other to total object status ("only a machine"), which truly negates the other as subject; (2) alienation of the other, which still therefore presupposes subjectivity. This second category may, for example, take the form of a master-slave relationship where only a quasi-subjectivity is granted.[14]

Can HAL ever be a "real" person? Not by our standard societal definition, for this does seem to require, among other things, embodiment in what we take to be a human form. Persons tend to be commonly conceived as a soul or mind *plus* body; we encountered something similar with Locke (concept of "man"), and it goes back at least to Plato. Of course this state of affairs could change if our conception of embodiment changed.[15]

In a face-to-face dialogue it is the other's "body" that speaks to me. The other's "body" becomes both the *site of narration* and the *site of ascription* for subjectivity. By this I mean that the subject, the "I" of the other's discourse, is attributed to a certain spatial location, the perceived origin of the voice. This physical body, the site of narration, thereby becomes endowed with the status of selfhood, becomes thereby a distinctly human body, a person rather than a mere impersonal mechanism or animal.[16] Even when the speaker is absent some form of ascription to an embodied authorial origin generally occurs. This act appears to be fundamental to our society.

The act of ascription of selfhood is a prime factor in the generation of what we call "persons," but it is also a factor in the formation of potentially troublesome concepts such as soul and mind. The soul (also the mind) has been traditionally viewed as distributed in the body in some way, though it is especially associated with the head and throat regions, both by the speaker and the addressee. William James points this out when he says that the spiritual self, or what is commonly taken for it, is really only those intimate and diffuse but continuous bodily motions or pressures occurring at the head and throat and does not necessarily indicate the presence of a soul substance. These motions are thus assumed to be the seat of the self, the feeling of subjectivity, or what James calls "the real nucleus of our personal identity."[17]

The head is the most obvious site of ascription for a personal self that originates primarily in voice (mouth and throat), and whose world is eminently visual (eyes). We must be careful, however, not to reify these so-called "spiritual" entities—soul, mind, self—and also not to set up unnecessary dualisms of mind and body substances. As we hope to have shown, the self (mind could also be included) is not a substance or thing at all; to consider it so would be to commit Ryle's category mistake. It is not therefore localizable in any but a derived sense. One becomes a subject for oneself, or one has a self, within a speech community where the "I" and "you" are played out. It is our inveterate habit of substantializing or reifying this "I," of giving it a being other than as expressed in the social praxis of discourse and at the moment of utterance, that leads us to the belief in localization and also, because it cannot of course be discovered at that locale (consider Descartes' glandular problem!), leads to an essential separability from the body. Ignoring the important functioning of language has created numerous such problems in the history of philosophy, problems that we are only now learning to look at from this new perspective—or simply to discard as totally ill-formed.

Signs of Derrida

Let us look more closely at the second misconception enumerated at the beginning of this chapter, particularly with a view to understanding further the nature of signification and meaning at the level of soliloquy—the "dialogue of the soul with itself." Soliloquy is especially important to the question of self-identity conceived narratologically and also to the function of shifters ("I," "you," "here," "there," "now," etc.). The second misconception can be formulated as follows: the belief in intentions or thoughts that exist prior to linguistic expression.

What is often supposed in ordinary discourse is that expression carries over in a communicative act what was initially given or known prelinguistically. This prelinguistic realm is considered to be a realm of thought or direct intuition that serves as a preconceptual origin and touchstone for the meaning and truth of our expressive utterances and statements. For perception this distinction is especially clear. I say "it is snowing outside," and this statement is presumably verified in my own perceptual experience and can be similarly verified by the addressee if he or she looks out the window. This position is essentially the one proposed by Edmund Husserl, whose phenomenology is one of its most detailed expressions. If we pursue Husserl's thought, primary in his earlier works, it will take us directly to a consideration of expression and soliloquy. We shall, in effect, be arguing against a Husserlian position.

For the early Husserl, the meaning (*Bedeutung*) of an expression is fulfilled in intuitive self-evidence or in the sense (*Sinn*) of extralinguistic experience, just as meaning may be taken as an expression of such a sense on the part of the speaker.[18] A prime function of expression, which requires a signifying medium, is thus to communicate a pregiven sense or *intended* content, a sense that is presumed to be directly present to oneself and which one seeks to indicate to others. Language (and we will take exception to this view) is then conceived of, in its ideal state, as a transparent or self-effacing conveyance of meaning from one interiority to another, from one "soul" to another. The goal of this communication is intuition, conceived of as the presence of the state of affairs (the referent) in itself, though one may of course remain at the level of meaning and simply accept the other's word. This latter situation is a very common practice; it indicates an important difference between meaning and truth. For Husserl, meaning is fulfilled in intuition, much as Kant's "empty" concepts are, or in the presence of the object intended (an object that could also be fictional or intellectual). It is with fulfillment that the truth of an utterance is directly attained.

There are a few distinctions to be made here. Signs may be broadly divided into two primary camps, which I shall call, following Husserl, "indicative" (or "indexical") and "expressive." The former functions like my pointing finger, or like smoke that indicates fire; no intermediary level of meaning is required; one simply has to know the ostensive convention or make the relevant association: "Every sign is a sign for something, but not every sign has 'meaning,' a 'sense' that the sign 'expresses.' "[19] Expressions, on the other hand, involve meaning, and are not therefore in a one-to-one relation to things. Expression *(Ausdruck)*, as in written and spoken language, operates through a degree of ideality; in fact, expressions refer in the first place to an ideality rather than to a reality. We can also say that expression expresses the meaning of things or states of affairs; it raises the sense of things to the level of communication.[20] Meaning thus requires the existence of a signifying medium (or legible structure) that allows for recognition and repetition of signification and meaning within a community. Without this *iterability* there could be no meaning, no communication from person A to person B.

It is essentially this iterability that allows meaning, and hence expression, to break with the empirical. "It is snowing," is meaningful whether it is snowing or not; it is meaningful now as later.[21] The ability of writing to communicate over centuries is a clear indication of this break, a break even from the moment and context of inscription and its psychological associations and implications.[22] Thus Derrida: "A written sign . . . is not exhausted in the present of its inscription."[23] It is of the essence of writing to be able, potentially, to transcend its particular context or site of production, to communicate in the absence of author, author's intention, and implied referential situation.

What is particularly problematic here is the presumption by expression theories of meaning to conceive of expression as a duplication or reproduction of a prior stratum—"to *repeat* or *duplicate* a sense content which does not wait for speech in order to be what it is," as Derrida says.[24] Expression is thus restricted to the model of communication, a communication of what is already prefigured in the interiority of consciousness and which is simply mirrored forth in the linguistic utterance. Truth then becomes a matter, on one side, of the adequacy of the expression to the intended sense and on the other of its adequacy to the object referred to. The dissociation that may occur with writing already points to a serious undermining of both these aspects of truth, and also of the conception of language as communication, that is, the passage of meaning from one soul to another.[25]

Already in Husserl's work, however, the notion of a neutral mirroring is problematic, for the expressed gives something of a new form to the preexpressed:

> A peculiar intentional instrument lies before us which essentially possesses the outstanding characteristic of reflecting back as from a mirror every other intentionality according to its form and content, of copying it whilst colouring it in its own way, and thereby of working into it its own form of "conceptuality." . . . Expression is not something like a coat of varnish or like a piece of clothing covering it over; it is a mental formation exercising new intentive functions on the intentive substratum. . . .[26]

More and more the initial instrumentality of language gives way to a creative function that generates rather than mirrors a pregiven meaning. But expression not only generates meaning, perhaps more importantly it also generates the subject and object (qua intended) *presupposed* by it. Was there in fact a subject preceding expression? This is a position that previous chapters have continually argued against. "There is," states Derrida, "no constituting subjectivity. The very concept of constitution itself must be deconstructed."[27] Let us now follow this constituting subject, necessarily presupposed by Husserl, back into soliloquy.

Expressions may rely on intuitive fulfilment for their *truth* value, but this is not what makes them *meaningful*. Meaning, as Saussure has pointed out, is a matter of the juxtaposition of traditional signs in a more or less grammatical chain (syntagm). Hence, even in interior "monologue" what one expresses may be quite meaningful. But the question to be faced concerns the communicative value of the expressions. Consider Husserl:

> One of course speaks, in a certain sense, even in soliloquy, and it is certainly possible to think of oneself as speaking, and even as speaking to oneself, as, e.g., when someone says to himself: 'You have gone wrong, you can't go on like that.' But in the genuine sense of communication, there is no speech in such cases, nor does one tell oneself anything. . . . In a monologue words can perform no function of indicating the existence of mental acts, since such indication would be quite purposeless. For the acts in question are themselves experienced by us at that moment.[28]

If, as Husserl claims, such communication is considered to be the expression of an already known intention, then communication to oneself is a gratuitous act. What follows from the act, what it indicates, is already present to oneself.[29] In order to follow this argument further let us turn briefly to the indexical function of expressions.

Expressions can, indeed must, be able to function also as indices. They may, for example, indicate attitudes, moods, or states of mind; bodily and facial "expressions" also do this.[30] Expression may also indicate the sheer otherness or the congeniality of the other. They may indicate the "intention" to describe a certain object, or a certain memory, feeling, or perception. They may further indicate a meaning that the speaker seems not aware of, and so on. These indicative functions are very often associations that experience teaches us, and they may also be subsidiary to the express meaning of the utterance.

The question to be faced is whether, qua listener, the speaker stands in a privileged relation to his own "thoughts," his own intentions, as Husserl would have us believe. Or is the speaker in the same position any other listener to such an utterance might be in? Does speech in general, like writing, also have a deferred or nonpresent origin? Is the subject produced in and through the signs, and not vice versa? It is significant that language is, to use Husserl's expression, interwoven (*verflochten*) with many other act strata.[31]

When people seek to express themselves do they really check, by something like a backward glance, with the preexpressed sense they seek to communicate? Does what is said never surprise the speaker? Is it not the case that the meaning, even the feel or tone, of the expression itself guides one's next utterance, by the way the utterance relates to the speech context for example? It appears to us that what one "intends" is not at all clearly given unless one has, or has had, the expression for it. It is usually only after the demonstrated inadequacy of an initial expression that one says "what I meant to say is . . . ," thus feeding in the intention after the fact.

Seeking an expression is very often a matter of attaining a degree of univocity, such that the expression cannot be taken wrongly by a listener. This seeking functions by exclusion and by knowing what one *has said* rather than what one supposedly "intended" to say. The adequacy of one's expression is a question of how one understands that expression oneself. If it is ambiguous, one rephrases it, and so on. It is interesting that when someone says "I have it on the tip of my tongue," they do not yet know what it is, do not yet have it, and they may only come to know what they "mean" in the moment of expression. It is as though the coming of language sets the sense free, brings it to the light of consciousness. Yet another example would be: "I know what I want to say, just give me time." How often it is that "what I wanted to say" gets worked out in the actual expressing.

These phenomena of language do not, I maintain, occur only in public speech but also in soliloquy. There is, to disagree with Husserl, no essential difference between the two. It is interesting to note, however, that in public one is often much more careful in one's formulations for they are questioned and corrected not only by oneself but, more importantly perhaps, by other people; that one in fact "does not know" becomes apparent more readily than in soliloquy. It can take discipline even to think in complete sentences to oneself.[32]

Rather than posit something like a private language or a privileged and mysterious self-knowledge, it is more economical (in Occam's sense) to suggest that in solitary monologue one's expressions first render the meanings of one's experiences or states present to oneself. This situation is not significantly different from expressing oneself to others. One essentially becomes an interlocutor to oneself.

Much of what I am saying here can be seen to derive from what was said in the preceding chapter, for it is especially clear in Taylor's description of the relation between emotion and expression. For Taylor, as we saw, man is defined as an interpreting animal, a language animal. It is this thorough embeddedness in language that is often overlooked by Husserl. We could also say it is because language and signification have already occurred that one has a "sense" of knowing beforehand. This phenomenon relates back to what I have called the prenarrative (quasi-narrative) level of our experience.

We can now take a further look at the language of the soliloquizing subject. Meaning is not a free-floating X but is indissolubly linked to a basis in materiality—to both the iterable mark on the paper and to the phonetic material of voice (e.g., one identifies the same word in different modulations of voice). It is this materiality of the sign that is iterable, that has a certain self-identity in its occurrences despite variations in voice and accent.[33] Ideality, to follow Derrida's lead, is a matter of the seemingly infinite repeatability of signs, their freedom from any particular utterance and any particular speaker. Ideality, therefore, does not properly apply to meaning, for meaning is thoroughly contextual and syntagmatically dependent.[34] In other words, meaning (where it is not what we commonly call "self-evident") is a matter of interpretation, where interpretation that seeks understanding is essentially an act of translating the given expression into what one sees to be an equivalent expression; it is putting the expression into one's own words, one's own language.[35]

Here we find another major indexical relationship: that existing between the materiality of the sign and the phenomenon of expressed meaning. One must see the vocal gestures or the written script as potentially meaningful, as indicating an "intention" toward meaning. It is especially the self-effacing nature of the phonetic medium that leads to our belief in something like an unmediated presence of meaning, to the belief in extra-linguistic sense (*Sinn*). It is as though the materiality of words immediately passes away once spoken, leaving behind the pure stratum of meaning, of which it was simply the carrier. But this is far from true. As Merleau-Ponty discovered,

> The wonderful thing about language is that it promotes its own oblivion: my eyes follow the lines on the paper, and from the moment I am caught up in their meaning, I lose sight of them. . . . Expression fades out before what is expressed, and this is why its mediating role may pass unnoticed. . . .[36]

"My words," writes Alfonso Lingis, "are 'living,' animate with my own life; they do not quit me, do not exteriorize themselves from my own breath."[37] Those iterable words that are always at my disposal are my lifeblood, for it is here that a certain self-consciousness arises and is constantly renewed in the form of hearing oneself speak. It is perhaps this relationship, which Derrida classes under acts of "auto-affection," that best founds our sense of subjectivity or self-consciousness. "This auto-affection," writes Derrida, "is no doubt the possibility for what is called *subjectivity* or the *for-itself* . . . without it, no world *as such* would appear."[38] Thus, if there is a presence of the subject to itself, it is the presence of the voice; it is here that I find myself expressed, where I hear myself expressed. The "I" appears in this auto-affective relation.[39]

The Alter Ego

If auto-affection is the possibility of subjectivity, this subjectivity finds its release, its expression of itself, in acts of signification. The feeling of subjectivity that we have more or less continually, I contend, is quite simply the possibility of signification, of expression, what might be called *vouloir dire* or a wanting and being able, in most cases, to say or express. But this subjectivity does not know itself outside the fulfillment of its desire to express.[40] It is at this level of desire that the use of the word *intention* becomes serviceable, but not as denoting some form of private language or transcendent subjectivity.

It is in the actual expression that I take my place as a subject among subjects; a place that is prepared by language itself. This preparation we have already seen in the function of personal pronouns, in the dialogical unity of "I" and "you." Just as the "I" gives voice to the silence of subjectivity, so "here" and "now" give voice and definition to my spatiotemporal being.[41] But what, we might ask, is the difference between the child who simply mimics the word *I* and the adult who expresses himself thereby? Before we can consider this question, we must distinguish between the casual user of the word and the one who, like Descartes, is philosophically fascinated by the "I," by the cogito.

The casual user is designated by the "I" but is not held by it; he or she is, rather, caught in the drift of the conversation and the topic at hand. The casual user is not usually concerned with what "I" actually means or what it indicates. As was said before, when one is asked what the "I" stands for, the common answer is some fairly vacuous variant on "me!" It usually takes either a philosophical mind or a significant event of some kind to prompt a further questioning of the "I." There are two types of questioning that can occur here. One is the explicitly philosophical kind that asks after "I-ness" in general; the other answers "who am I?" in terms of an autobiographical or narrative account.[42] In earlier chapters we were focusing primarily on the second narrational type of questioning; here we are pursuing the philosophical question ourselves.

When the child mimics the saying of "I" he may be on the way to authentic expression (wherein the speaking subject identifies with the subject of speech), but insofar as his vocalization only mimics the phonetic material this gesture can be considered no differently than other sounds he makes; it is neither an expression nor normal speech. The first vocal gestures of a young child are on a par with the spontaneous gestures of his limbs. Such gestures are indices and not true expressions (as these were defined in relation to Husserl), and are to be interpreted in a scheme of associations. It is only from the second year and later that the child is capable of clearly distinguishing his own person and his own perspective from that of others, while allowing others their own perspective. As Merleau-Ponty has written,

> The pronoun *I* has its full meaning only when the child uses it not as an individual sign to designate his own person—a sign that would be assigned once and for all to himself and to nobody else—but when he understands that each person he sees can in turn say *I* that each person is an *I* for himself and a *you* for others.[43]

It is perhaps true, however, that if the child had no prelinguistic sense of self (no matter how vague), he could not develop into that which language offers him. It will therefore be of use here to outline what Jacques Lacan calls the "mirror stage," for it presents us with a prototypical situation of I-identification at an age preceding language acquisition.[44]

Lacan distinguishes between what he calls the *symbolic,* the *imaginary,* and the *real* in human experience. The first two realms are defined primarily in opposition to the real or that which is always outside representation and signification. The real is analogous to the drives and desires that, in Freudian theory, are "tamed" by civilization; it also approximates a mute nature in the nature-culture split.[45] Both the imaginary (images, perceptions) and the symbolic may serve in the formation of a "subject," but the symbolic is the primary order.

Language is, for Lacan, the privileged symbolic medium, but symbolization extends to rituals, ceremonies, conventions, and such like. By "symbol" Lacan means the realm of signification generative of meaning through a system of differential relations (much as Saussure defined language). Entry into the symbolic begins with the acquisition of language, and from that point on, says Lacan, the real is gradually left behind. Reality is, as it were, redefined and alienated in the new social and cultural order of the symbolic:

> Symbols . . . envelop the life of man in a network so total that they join together, before he comes into the world, those who are going to engender him "by flesh and blood"; so total that they bring to his birth . . . the shape of his destiny; so total that they give the words that will make him faithful or renegade, the law of the acts that will follow him right to the very place where he is not yet and even beyond his death. . . .[46]

The symbolic is thus where the child, as a member of a family unit of such and such a type, is constituted even before it is born. Becoming the subject of this symbolic prefiguration (i.e., becoming what it signifies) is one of the child's passions as well as one of its torments, and is well documented, for example, in many novels that deal with the problem of finding one's own identity against the impositions of others.

The symbolic does not directly represent or correspond to the real, for it generates a level of signification, and therefore meaning, in a more or less closed network of mutual relations that both refigure and transcend the level of the real. This mutual relation of signifiers is such that the signified is always another element in the signifying network, that is, another signifier or group of signifiers. (It is to this symbolic realm that Benveniste's account of the subject truly belongs.) Lacan accordingly sees in the expressions of subjectivity a split that is symptomatic of this real-symbolic division, a split between the embodied speaking subject (real) and the subject as signified in, say, language (symbolic). This latter division is essentially what we have already argued for in terms of the division between the *speaking subject* and the *subject of speech.* The embodied subject, in effect, is externalized in language (and in other signifying systems) and identifies with the externalization, the projection.[47] This stage of identification is productive of what we will call the *spoken subject,* the final stage of the linguistic auto-affective relation.

This alienation of the symbolic from the real is best exemplified in the earlier "mirror stage" of imaginary representation. The young child is thought to have no conception of itself (in the linguistic sense of concept), and its bodily image of itself (if it can be said to have one) is at first highly fragmented into the various auto-affective relations pertaining to its own bodily functions, particularly the touching-touched relation. Unlike its perception of others, who may have a certain visual totality, the child is presumed to have no vantage point from which to view itself in a like manner. Some form of visual reflection corrects this deficit.

Lacan contends that the mirror stage occurs first at about the age of six months.[48] It involves the child's identifying with its specular body image:

> This jubilant assumption of his specular image by the child at the *infans* stage, still sunk in his motor incapacity and nursling dependence, would seem to exhibit in an exemplary situation the symbolic matrix in which the I is precipitated in primordial form, before it is objectified in the dialectic of identification with the other, and before language restores to it, in the universal, its function as subject.

What this experience, which is essentially that of objectification, yields is a visual or imaginary (in Lacan's sense; not to be equated with fanciful) *alter ego* set over against oneself, one's bodily feeling being, that one then identifies with. Correlative to this development in the imaginary there is also a significant reorganization of the child's spatial field in relation to this newfound "sense" of self. Says Lacan, "the mirror-image would seem to be the threshold of the visible world." One important effect of this imago is a break in the syncretic identification with others around him, a separation of his life and actions from theirs.

Important here is that the mirror image is not experienced as separate from the child's identity, and yet it is a displacement from the immediacy of the tactile body (the real). Lacan locates this *méconnaissance* at the origin of self-consciousness, and its general structure of displacement (the "fragmented body") is carried through into the symbolic stage. From the narcissism of the mirror stage, for example, the infant gradually transfers its ego ideal onto other people, especially the mother. The symbolic does not, however, totally replace the imaginary, for the identification, say, with iconic role models and ideals continues throughout life.[49] Consider in this regard the seductive effects of advertising and films, and also the quasi-presence that one experiences in front of photographs and the like. In many societies the imago is potentially dangerous (as is one's name) if it gets into the wrong hands. The mirror stage is highly indicative of the role that representation of oneself (doubling-mimesis) will play throughout one's cultural life, and of which narrative recounting is a primary form.

We can see in Lacan's account of the mirror stage a few traits that we have noted before. The I or ego is not the product of a gradually evolving, self-generating consciousness, as though self-consciousness simply enlarges itself from itself in the course of the child's experiencing. There is in the mirror stage a fundamental dialectic with an other that precludes such an autonomy of consciousness. As Lacan points out, we should not "regard the ego as centered on the perception-consciousness system, or as organized by the 'reality principle'—a principle that is the expression of a scientific prejudice most hostile to the dialectic of knowledge." Rather should we start "from the function of *méconnaissance* that characterizes the ego in all its structures. . . ."[50]

Merleau-Ponty proposed a similar view when he considered the child's perception of others: "the perception of others cannot be accounted for if one begins by supposing an ego and another that are absolutely conscious of themselves, each of which lays claim, as a result, to an *absolute* originality in relation to the other that confronts it."[51] Merleau-Ponty's role of the body image and the *image speculaire* in the initial relation of a child to the other, and to itself, perfectly parallels the function of Lacan's mirror stage.

The specular I and the general structure of consciousness that it maps out represent a loss of presence, especially if we equate presence with a unity of being that overlaps with itself, that is transparent to itself and knows itself as origin. If Lacan's category of the real stands for something like an originary self-enclosed being, this is not a form of being that has self-presence. Only by the detour of the other is self-presence attained. Earlier I noted that Ricoeur, in his account of hermeneutics, also insists on some such detour if self-knowledge is to be had. As we have seen, this self-presence is precisely a presence grounded in an identity given through difference. This conclusion relates back especially to the illusions of intentions and of the supposed thinker behind the thinking.

Let us now draw some of our conclusions together. Our investigations up to this point reveal a subject that can be conceived, and can "conceive" of itself, in a number of ways. Each of these ways is related to certain concrete experiences; they are not intellectual abstractions. There is, first of all, the "I am I" experience of syncretic unity (in the child this is primarily characterized by "introspective" feelings and impulses). Second, there is the auto-affective stage prior to the mirror stage, where no stable or holistic self-identification occurs. Third, there is the mirror stage, which sets up, on the plane of the imaginary, a representational self-image that the child identifies with. Fourth, beyond the mirror stage comes the realm of role models that the image identification is transferred to; one gains selfhood in and through other persons. Finally, through the acquisition of language there is a gradual and complex identification with voice, thought, and abstraction on the plane of the symbolic. This identification is based especially on the speaking-hearing dyad, which, in expressions of meaning, promotes the belief in an interiority of consciousness or, in a word, *mind.* The assumption of a substantial self behind expression occurs partly by overlooking the essential materiality of the signifier.

The symbolic level also opens positions prefigured for the subject in the form of personal pronouns, and these have been shown (in the first person) to be dialectical. In interior monologue this dialectic still occurs—in the form of talking to oneself. Here the alienation, or duplicity, of the mirror stage continues. One may still ask: "Is the I that speaks the same as the I spoken about?" With this entry into language proper (the symbolic) all other modes of I-identification tend to fall prey to the linguistic and to the type of understanding that the linguistic affords. Only perhaps in dreams and "mental" disorders do we find what seems to be a predominance of the more archaic modes.

It is often considered important, in matters pertaining to self-consciousness and self-understanding, that the relation of the preexpressed and the expressed is such that the latter should mirror the former. But we have seen that this model disregards the essential relation of ourselves to language. The disclosive power of language is formative of the subject,[52] of a speaking subject that defines itself in its own expressions and identifies with the subject there portrayed. Earlier chapters have sought to delineate the preexpressed or prenarrative realm in terms of both the prior functioning of language and the quasi-narrative structure characteristic of experience itself. We have seen that the prenarrative nature of experience serves as a basis for interpretive narrational activity (as for recollection), but such narration cannot be said to aim simply at mirroring the prenarrative level. We shall now consider, taking psychoanalysis as an example, what is meant by saying that narrative can be the *truth* of the prenarrative.

Narrative and Truth

> The problem of recognizing oneself is the problem of recovering the ability to recount one's own history.
>
> Paul Ricoeur
> "The Question of Proof in Freud's Psychoanalytic Writings"

An important question that arises from the contemporary emphasis on the self as a narrative construct concerns the adequacy or truthfulness of the narrative accounts we give of ourselves. What, for example, stops our self-narrations and self-characterizations from becoming, in many cases, mere inauthentic flights of fancy or sheer fictions? If, on a fairly radical view, the self is taken to be a product of narrative emplotment, then clearly this question cannot be answered by a simple appeal to what the narrative is supposed to copy or represent—as though the self were first given to us outside or prior to the narrative. It is not immediately clear, however, just what a narrative account of the human subject could be adequate to; and if we were to grant some prenarrative status to the human subject, it is also not clear whether the imposition of narrative structures falsifies the "truth" of this latter subject. What we shall examine here, then, is precisely this important question of adequacy and various problems that surround it.

Guiding our present investigation is this question: to what degree can the truthfulness of a self-narration be considered more a matter of pragmatic and creative adequacy than of a correspondence to the way things actually were or are? We have already seen, in my treatment of memory, that although the past is a constant horizon and support for the present, it is not thereby given with fullness of meaning to reflection and recollection. Recollection, I maintained, is both selective and interpretive. We do indeed remember that certain events have occurred, but understanding their import implies the further task of discerning a chain of events or a story to which they belong.

Self-understanding also requires that we see some form of causality (and rationality) operating in our lives. For human actions this causality takes the form of motivations or purposes. In *The Phenomenology of the Social World,* Alfred Schutz makes a useful division of human motivation into two aspects: the "because-of" and the "in-order-to" motives. The former motive is oriented to the past, while the latter is futural. Understanding human action necessarily involves the explication of these two aspects of motivation. Without the meaning conferred by such an explication we would have, at best, only a chronicle of events.[53]

A central problem with motivation is its not being fully conscious to the actor. Motivational contexts usually extend beyond anything we explicitly formulate, and part of the reason for this is simple forgetfulness. How often have we read in a novel something like this: "Although he didn't know it yet, it was his growing love for her that drove him to such extremes of behavior." Other problems with describing motives concern the possibility for fabrication and duplicity. For example, one's explicit reasons for acting can disguise a deeper, less conscious motive. This disguised motive may also be the product of repression, say, rather than just a simple oversight.

Perhaps the very suggestion of fully accounting for motives is in the end doomed to failure or is at least highly problematic, for such a task would seem to require a foundational subject that has the sources of its own acts potentially within scrutiny. The meaning of our acts, however, as this is worked out in terms of because-of and in-order-to motives, is a product of retrospective and prospective emplotments that draw upon the prenarrative past, refiguring it in light of the present demand for sense and coherence. Here again we find the dialectic of the prenarrative and narrative, a dialectic that is, to borrow a useful phrase from Merleau-Ponty, one of *creative adequation.*

This dialectical situation places us in the proverbial chicken-or-egg dilemma—the hermeneutical resolution of which is to say that we cannot have one without the other. We undoubtedly act based on our prenarrative context, but the question of motivations immediately involves us, as self-conscious human subjects, in our awareness and expression of such motivations. As human subjects we not only act but do so within a more or less detailed plan or emplotment of the action. The question of "truth" thus involves us in the question of the adequacy with which our explicit narrations map onto or otherwise follow from prenarrative experience.

As stated, however, this approach involves us in the problematic epistemological stance of a correspondence theory of truth. The correspondence theory is, however, only tenable if our prenarrative experience has meaning for us outside our interpretations or emplotment of it, but, as I have argued in this and earlier chapters, such is not the case. The truth of our narratives does not reside in their correspondence to the prior meaning of prenarrative experience; rather, *the narrative is the meaning of prenarrative experience.* The adequacy of the narrative cannot, therefore, be measured against the meaning of prenarrative experience but, properly speaking, only against alternate interpretations of that experience.[54]

Our task here, then, is to pursue what is meant by a creative adequation between prenarrative and narrative experience, with the emphasis on the word *creative.* To illuminate this relationship I shall begin by taking a further look at psychoanalysis and conclude with an examination of historical writing.

If the telos of the symbolic, as we saw earlier from Lacan, is to generate a subject whose domain is in the order of signification, this transformation must occur at the expense of what he calls the *real*: drives, instincts, primary desires (keyed especially to the sites of bodily processes, but also to external objects of intimacy and gratification), and the body's rhythms generally. This symbolic subject is always on the way to becoming the Cartesian subject or Husserlian transcendental ego that, from the secure platform of the cogito, is assured of its own unity, homogeneity, and epistemic centrality. What holds the symbolic subject back, what checks its flight, are the transgressions wrought by the more "primitive" level. As Julia Kristeva says, "anguish, frustration, identification or projection all break down the unity of the transcendental ego and its system of homogeneous sense and give free rein to what is heterogeneous in sense, that is, to the drive [*Trieb*]." In such transgressions, especially if they are extreme, "the speaking subject undergoes a transition to a void, to zero: loss of identity, afflux of drive and a return of symbolic capacities, but this time in order to take control of drive itself."[55]

This shift, Kristeva contends, is what inaugurates new signifying processes, particularly of a creative or poetic kind. Poetic language with its reliance on metaphor and metonymy is, in its revitalizing of our symbolic capacities, essentially a revolutionary practice, overturning the categories with which we commonly describe ourselves.[56] What poetic discourse (especially lyric) establishes, to borrow from Kristeva, is a subject-in-process, a subject still finding or refiguring itself. This unsettled subject manifests itself as a speaking subject that diverges from normal referential and communicative discourse. In this respect, poetic discourse often operates, much like Freud's discourse of the unconscious, through displacements and condensations that may defy both semantic and grammatical categorial interpretations.[57] What "speaks" in such instances is a state of being anterior to the Cartesian subject. What is said may be epistemically unprecedented.[58]

Whereas poetic discourse gives willing voice to otherwise unformed desires and emotions, that which is repressed seeks a voice for what the conscious subject has, for one reason or another, avoided or put aside. In operation these two processes can be very similar.[59] Lacan states the psychoanalytic model as follows:

> Undoubtedly, something that is not expressed does not exist. But the repressed is always there—it insists, and it demands to come into being. The fundamental relation of man with this symbolic order is precisely the same one which founds this symbolic order itself—the relation of being to non-being.
>
> That which insists on being satisfied can only be satisfied through recognition. The end of the symbolic process is that non-being comes to be, that he is because he has spoken.[60]

For Lacan the unconscious develops from the split that the symbolic introduces into our being. The unconscious thus evolves dialectically with the expressed; it is the other side, as it were, of the expressed. In this way, as Lacan says, "the unconscious is structured like a language"—a phrase that might usefully be said of prenarrative experience generally.[61]

The origin of this view is found in Freud's notion of unconscious "dream-thoughts" that undergo transformation and censorship in the dream-work and which interpretation seeks to uncover.[62] Psychoanalysis is thus a process of disclosing the "discourse" of the unconscious that motivates and subverts our explicit discourse, particularly our self-narrations, and this means (at least for Lacan) being sensitive to the metaphoric and metonymic transformations that occur as this other discourse enters conscious expression. In psychoanalytic practice the analysand should come to recognize and appropriate this other discourse; this may be seen as the central moment of "curing" the analysand. As Lacan succinctly puts it, "Analysis can have for its goal only the advent of a true speech and the realization by the subject of his history in his relation to a future."[63]

It should be clear how this model of the subject fits in with our previous discussions of the prenarrative level.[64] The psychoanalytic prenarrative is a part of one's own history, one's experience, that is refused anything but an oblique entry into one's ongoing and conscious life story. Though it has its roots in a perhaps instinctual bodily basis, this prenarrative nevertheless has conscious recognition as its goal and is already a structuring force in one's self-conception. What psychoanalysis is premised upon and constantly stresses is the resistance of the subject to its own truth: "One is never happy making way for a new truth," says Lacan, "for it always means making our way into it; the truth is always disturbing."[65]

Earlier we talked of this truth of the subject in terms of an act of creative adequation, and this tends to involve, at least in the psychoanalytic case, overcoming prior and perhaps well-established interpretations of ourselves. This is also a reason why literature, at its best, is both disturbing and liberating. We shall now pursue this notion of truth a little further, keeping psychoanalysis as our guide.

Psychoanalysis is known as the "talking cure" precisely because its analyses are carried out primarily in the realm of discourse and dialogue—the discourse of the analysand with himself and with the analyst. It has become increasingly evident that a primary aim of the analyst is the unfolding of a life history, a history that does justice both to the past and to the present. Analysis can take diverse routes, but the end result is a narrative account of the analysand's life wherein the analysand finds him or herself adequately reflected and can accept this representation as biographical and, perhaps more fruitfully, as a basis for future action. As Roy Schafer writes, "It has been becoming increasingly clear in recent years that clinical psychoanalysis is an interpretative discipline whose concern it is to construct life histories of human beings."[66] Why this should be so is that the human subject, as we have stressed, exists and knows itself as the implied subject of its own discourse and narratives (though often these are told by other people). "We are," says Schafer, "forever telling stories about ourselves. In saying that we also tell them *to ourselves,* however, we are enclosing one story within another. This is the story that there is a self to tell something to, a someone else serving as audience who is oneself or one's self."[67]

We have already discussed this self in terms of the implied subject (especially signified by the personal pronouns) and the speaking-listening dyad. What Schafer is pointing to is that the reality of the subject for itself is primarily linguistic, derived from its self-narrations. Schafer rightly applies this thesis also to other persons: "The other person, like the self, is not something one has or encounters as such but is an existence one tells."[68] Even where this story of other persons is not explicitly told there is, nevertheless, the implicit assumption that it could be told.

Let us consider an example from neuropsychology. In *The Man Who Mistook His Wife for a Hat,* Oliver Sacks discusses various cases of memory disorders caused by Korsakoff's syndrome. Of one patient with a memory span of only a few seconds, Sacks notes:

> Unable to maintain a genuine narrative or continuity, unable to maintain a genuine inner world, he is driven to the proliferation of pseudo-narratives, in a pseudo-continuity, pseudo-worlds peopled by pseudo-people, phantoms.

Such a patient, says Sacks, "must literally make himself (and his world) up every moment." The problem here is that memory loss makes it impossible to link different narrative instances around a common theme or development, and yet some sort of narrative is necessary for a sense of identity and purpose. The identity of the patient, for himself, can only be maintained through continuous narrative activity, through staging dramas in each succeeding moment: "The world keeps disappearing, losing meaning, vanishing—and he must seek meaning, *make* meaning, in a desperate way, continually inventing, throwing bridges of meaning over abysses of meaninglessness. . . ." For the patient these bridges are not mere inventions; they are the world as he knows it, as he interprets it at that moment, and the same will apply to his sense of selfhood.[69]

What this example illustrates is both the ongoing need for narrating experience in order to exist *as* a meaningful human subject and the function of narrative in generating a continuity of identity, of self. Indeed, a good case can be made for viewing narrative understanding as the most adequate approach to the human domain. To understand ourselves we must grasp our own implicit history, for to be human is not simply to have a history (in a certain sense animals have this), but to be cognizant of this history. This is why the "linguistic turn" of hermeneutics, unlike much of Anglo-American language philosophy, goes hand in hand with narration and therefore with historical analysis and description.

The continuity afforded by narrative, however, can be a feigned one—especially from the perspective of other people. Sacks's patient had no knowledge of his dispersed self other than through the reports given by other people. The narratives he invented were simply fragments or residues of his past life and past occupations (his fragmented habitus), which were then arbitrarily imposed on the present. These stories (and dramas) were created (and acted out) by the patient not only to give himself a role to play but also to integrate his surroundings into something familiar, something that makes sense. Socially, however, the identity he created was a failure, for there was an imposition of roles on other people that were simply not appropriate and an adoption of roles by the patient that, for an observer, were absurd or misplaced.

Because of the physical damage to his brain, Sacks's patient could not be cured of his delusory fabrications; anything told to him was forgotten after a brief interval and the fabrications began anew. Such a person lives at the level of shifting surface phenomena. He lacks the depth, the richness, and the constraints that the past usually imposes on one. Psychoanalysis, on the other hand, is aimed at people who have the possibility of augmenting their life stories in light of present practices and expectations as well as their past. But there are numerous interpretive barriers to be encountered—and not only, for example, in the recounting of dreams, for even in the narrating of what took place yesterday there are problems of interpretive distortion to be overcome.

As we saw earlier, even memory retrieval involves a degree of emplotment if what is remembered is to be interpreted and understood in the context of an ongoing life.[70] The psychoanalytic analysand has the additional problem of the involuntary masking of certain events and interpretations. Certain avenues of interpretation of the past may be closed or inhibited because of traumatic experience in the past, for example.[71] The analyst is especially seeking to facilitate the movement of such repressed contents into explicit speech and recognition. But here again there is an interpretive problem. Analysts must interpret what is told to them out of their own interpretive schemes, with consideration of a direction the analysis is to take and on the basis of their own life experiences. The problems multiply when we consider the stories involved in the psychoanalytic dialogue.

There is, first of all, the presumed story "waiting to be told" which contains the key to anomalies or inconsistencies in one's present behavior; this is the repressed story, and it belongs at the prenarrative level. Second, there is the story told by the analysand. This story may be a pure fabrication, but even if it is a report of what the analysand distinctly remembers there will still be, in the telling, impositions of both style and context onto what is told, as well as selectivity. Also, in Habermasian terms, one will likely understand out of an "interest." Thus the so-called facts are told in a certain manner, style, or genre, and for certain effects, to illuminate certain points, and also out of certain interests that inform the dialogical situation. And no doubt there could be other factors involved that we have not mentioned, such as one's emotional state during the telling. Third, there may be the further story which the analysand constructs on the basis of his or her initial disclosure. This latter story would be the story of what the story told "actually means" to the analysand upon reflection. Fourth, there is the story as heard by the analyst, the meaning of which is inevitably different from the analysand's, for it is heard against a different background, out of a different context and interests. Finally, there is the underlying story that the analyst seeks behind what is told—the subtext. In classic psychoanalytical theory, which Freud saw as an archaeology, this latter story should coincide with the first story, the repressed story which is the "truth" of the analysand's past.[72] What, then, are we to make of the above proliferation of narratives?

Truth, as the term is commonly used, relates to the adequacy of statements for conveying the way things actually were or are. The archeological model of psychoanalysis would similarly commit one to what might be called "historical truth": the correspondence of descriptions to the analysand's past. What has become evident to numerous psychoanalysts, however, is that this historical truth is little more than "narrative truth." As Donald Spence remarks, it "is more appropriate to think of construction than reconstruction; to give up the archaeological model; to think of an interpretation as a pragmatic statement that has no necessary referent in the past; and to replace historical truth by narrative truth."[73] In other words, the archaeological-historical method commits one to a merely factual view about a person's past, thereby reducing the contextual significance of the present and future for the very meaning of the past. The archaeological model seeks story number one (above) as though it were fully formed and had only to be brought to consciousness and recognized for what it is. Such a view, as we saw in the chapter on time and memory, disregards the futural nature of human existence and the hermeneutic dimension of interpretation. The past has meaning only in light of what precedes it and what follows it (Schutz's because-of and in-order-to motives). This requirement is what makes all recollection that seeks understanding a narrative endeavor, a matter of emplotment. Story number one is only a quasi-narrative, a story still to be told, and told from a certain perspective.

Much of the past, including motivations and possible complexes, is only on the way to language, and the carry-over is often a rather difficult, creative, and prolonged task (if psychoanalysis is anything to go by!). As Spence maintains, "The construction not only shapes the past—it *becomes* the past in many cases because many critical early experiences are preverbal and, therefore, have no proper designation until we put them into words."[74]

The analysand's explicit associations and recollections are like so much disorganized material that needs to be understood in light of a narrative that holds it together in a development that yields familiarity, meaning, and, accordingly, understanding. This is a process that in our ordinary lives we commonly achieve satisfactorily. The methodological result to be gleaned from this is that psychoanalysts should not orient themselves toward revealing a final story that supposedly duplicates a repressed past but should enable the analysand to overcome problems in the present by allowing the formation of a therapeutic narrative that nevertheless gives meaning and direction to the analysand's life.

Narrative truth is thus more a matter of facilitating understanding and integration than of generating strict historical verisimilitude (supposing this were even possible at our level of investigation). To quote Spence again:

> Narrative truth can be defined as the criterion we use to decide when a certain experience has been captured to our satisfaction; it depends on continuity and closure and to the extent to which the fit of the pieces takes on an aesthetic finality. . . . Once a given construction has acquired narrative truth, it becomes just as real as any other kind of truth.[75]

Spence's last remark may appear somewhat extreme, but one must remember the context within which it is written. When dealing with the meaning of a person's life (or of the past) we can only have interpretations that, given what we otherwise know of that life, afford us a satisfactory comprehension of it (especially of motives). As I argued earlier, interpretations vie for credibility not simply in their accounting for the known details of a life but, more importantly, in relation to other and perhaps more viable interpretations. Spence's use of the term *real* may still be puzzling, but what is implied is that a narrative account that fulfills the conditions he mentions (continuity, closure, etc.) is the optimum in our understanding of a person's life. That is, the historical account must become narrational if a comprehensive understanding of individual lives is the goal.

While one may agree with Spence's general position, it should be noted that certain questions are nevertheless raised by his account. First, there is the problem of the relativism of narrative interpretations. No one account can be regarded as *the* final truth. This is, however, a limited relativism, for there will exist extranarrative elements (e.g., knowing that, in relation to dates, and places) for which one seeks a narrative emplotment. Presumably the narrative must respect both the temporal sequence of these elements and their content, and it must also link them in a way that is intellectually and emotionally acceptable. The narrative should, in other words, provide a feasible context for the exhibiting of the elements in their causal and temporal connections and should reveal how the past is operating on the present and on the expected future (though perhaps with apprehension). As Spence indicates, the final judgement of a narrative is its acceptance by the one whose experience it recounts and whose reflected life it becomes, even though this acceptance may not be easily won. It should also be noted that one's own acceptance of a narrative may be significantly affected by whether or not other people accept one's account.

Another possible problem with narrative relates to its aesthetic and rhetorical appeal. Once certain experiences are brought into some form of narrative sequence and closure there may be a tendency to accept uncritically the finished product. This situation is due primarily to the persuasive rhetorical character of narratives. A related problem is that any series of events may be amenable to numerous and different tellings, to different ways of filling in the gaps left by recollection. This question of open-ended interpretation is, however, common not only to self-understanding but to all fields of the humanities and cannot be avoided.

The kind of truth proposed here is, as Spence mentions, a pragmatic one. Psychologically, narrative is aimed not at achieving a mirror image of one's history but at generating a plausible account of the details of that history and allowing one to have an understanding of oneself that facilitates the overcoming of psychic blockages and allows one to function satisfactorily in the present. In fact, a fictional narrative could serve the same end if it addressed the right questions, situations, and conflicts. As C. G. Jung stated at the beginning of his autobiography, "Whether or not the stories are 'true' is not the problem. The only question is whether what I tell is my fable, my truth."[76] We are after all story-telling animals, speaking as much in allusions, symbols, and metaphors as in the logic of "objective facts." Narrative truth is thus a matter of adequacy and fit to what is otherwise given, and this is so not only for psychoanalysis but also for historiography and any form of recollection that seeks to unfold a past history that aims at more than a mere chronology.

We turn now to a broader discussion of historical narrative in general, especially with a view to addressing the ideological distortions that always threaten self-narration.

Like self-narration, the writing of history is a way of consolidating a past, a tradition, and therefore an identity. Like self-narration, history is also concerned with a form of archaeology that operates on a prenarrative subtext, though in this case the prenarrative material consists primarily of material artifacts in addition to memorial traces. However, both self-narration and history writing have a common grounding in the sense of our lives as being temporally circumscribed.

In much the same way that contemporary philosophy has brought into question the status of an underlying self or soul substance and has, as I have done here, sought to approach an understanding of the human subject via the paradigm of language, so many historiographers and philosophers of history have problematized historical research by investigating the nature and presuppositions of the historian's use of both language and narrative. The dream of a history which, in Ranke's words, reports the past *wie es eigentlich gewesen* becomes questioned.[77] History, considered hermeneutically, is an interpretive discipline that should not hope to coincide with past events but must make do, as the French historiographer Paul Veyne contends, with narrative reconstructions in language: "Knowledge of the past is not an immediate datum, for history is an area in which there can be no intuition but only reconstruction."[78]

Given that history writing is a narrative endeavor,[79] akin to the novel, we are led to ask after the status of its "referent." Hayden White states the problem in this way:

> the problem of narrativity turns on the issue of whether historical events can be truthfully represented as manifesting the structures and processes of those met with more commonly in certain kinds of "imaginative" discourses, that is, such as fictions. . . .[80]

If we consider this question from the point of view of a form-content distinction, it is an easy matter to say that *formally* historical discourse borrows from literature, but that nevertheless its *content* is drawn from "reality" rather than from the imagination. That is, the content of history is found rather than invented; its final referent is not simply a product immanent to one's narrative, but is external to the recounted story.

The answer I have already formulated to this question of reference is, on the contrary, that narrativity is a principle of intelligibility and not simply a vehicle for a pregiven and evident sense. As I have argued, the given (human actions, transactions, and so on) has a quasi-narrative status that has yet to be brought to explicit narrative understanding. This latter process, however, will not tolerate a description in terms of a simplistic dichotomy of form and content. Narrative expression is not mere communication of information but is a constitutive and synthetic activity. Historical narration takes its lead from artifacts but must aim beyond them to a synthesis that yields a satisfactory coherence, directionality, and intelligibility; otherwise history would be a mere cataloguing or dating and could not hope to rise beyond the chronicle stage. Peter Gay says as much when he writes: "Historical narration without analysis is trivial, historical analysis without narration is incomplete."[81]

What historical narrative generates is not a neutral mirror of the past but a seeing of the past *as* something: as a gradual emancipation from certain class structures, as an unfolding tragedy, as dominated by certain religious beliefs, etc. The artifacts may be seen to justify such interpretations or stories, but they can usually be seen to justify numerous other stories as well. As with recollection, present interest and the conceptual tools of the present set parameters to what material will be deemed relevant, what story will be told and the style (or genre) of that story. Hayden White makes a similar point in his collection of essays *Tropics of Discourse:*

> Histories are not only about events but also about the possible sets of relationships that those events can be demonstrated to figure. These sets of relationships are not, however, immanent in the events themselves; they exist only in the mind of the historian reflecting on them. Here they are present as the modes of relationships conceptualized in the myth, fable, and folklore, scientific knowledge, religion, and literary art, of the historian's own culture.

> But more importantly, they are . . . immanent in the very language which the historian must use to *describe* events prior to a scientific analysis of them or a fictional emplotment of them."[82]

The unavoidable and hermeneutical "seeing as" of historical narrative is what gives to the fragments of the past a significance beyond their mere occurrence.

But of course the historical past generally does not consist of mere disparate events and archival material. The past is, for most societies at least, already historicized, already told and continually updated. As with our self-narrations, one's present account is largely a reworking of stories already related, already participated in—only the amnesiac begins, as it were, *ab nuovo*. As we noted earlier, experience is irredeemable qua experience and, in addition, it is the significance or meaning of the experience and the world that one seeks to present and understand via narration.[83]

This intertextual and literary nature of historical narration has not been overlooked in contemporary scholarship. Roland Barthes, for example, goes so far as to bring historical narrative and fictional narrative into the same camp, with a view to contesting the former's claim to scientificity and objectivity:

> Does the narration of past events, which, in our culture from the time of the Greeks onwards, has generally been subject to the sanction of historical "science," bound to the underlying standard of the "real," and justified by the principle of "rational" exposition—does this form of narration really differ, in some indubitably distinctive feature, from imaginary narration, as we find it in the epic, the novel, and the drama?[84]

The object of Barthes's criticism is twofold: a rejection of extralinguistic referentiality and a critique of the ideological use of historical discourse. We can go along with both criticisms, but only to a certain degree.

Barthes sums up his rejection of reference in this way:

> Claims concerning the "realism" of narrative are therefore to be discounted. . . . The function of narrative is not to "represent," it is to constitute a spectacle. . . . Narrative does not show, does not imitate. . . . "What takes place" in a narrative is from the referential (reality) point of view literally *nothing*; "what happens" is language alone, the adventure of language. . . .[85]

This claim is aimed at narrative in general; although it may appear to apply primarily to literary fictions, it is nevertheless, for Barthes, also applicable to historical discourse.

Barthes's principal point here is that the meaning of a narrative is a product of its language and thus cannot be said to mirror the nature of "real," extralinguistic, past events. In historical discourse we construct a spectacle that via the authority of its author (its academic situation, and so on) is deemed "historical" and is thereby granted a referentiality to the "real" world—much as the implied subject of a personal narrative is reified into an existent soul substance, a thing. Like Mink ("Stories are not lived but told"), Barthes views narrative as an integrative way in which the past is given a meaning it otherwise lacks, a meaning that is actually a play of language that is far from ideologically innocent in its "recounting": "As we can see, simply from looking at its structure . . . historical discourse is in its essence a form of ideological elaboration."[86]

Such historical narratives have a performative dimension that often serves surreptitiously to fashion and promote a certain image of man. One has only to consider mythological world views to appreciate how the individual's image of himself and his social relations are delimited and perhaps constrained by the parameters placed on his "reality" by the society's "histories." In our own time, histories differ depending on whether they are told by the East or the West, the rich or the poor, them or us.

I have already said a good deal about the illocutionary force of narratives in chapter 2. However, what is overlooked in Barthes's strongly semiological-structural account is that narrative expression is constantly interwoven with what he calls "reality." There is still in Barthes a dichotomy of the narrated (language) and the real (nonlinguistic reality). If this "real" is consistently examined, however, we find that it cannot be exempted from at least a quasi narrativity (this was my argument against Mink). Historical narratives, like their personal counterparts, need not be free floating but, as I have said, can draw on the narrative structure of human time itself, on the story that is already evidenced in the purposive structure of human events.

Historical discourse, like self-narration, falls into that intermediary realm between fact and fiction; this is what leads Paul Veyne to say that "history is a true novel."[87] What *distinguishes* history from fiction is that the events related in the former are presumed to have actually taken place and were, at the time, witnessed or undergone by certain real persons. An additional factor is that the historian is often concerned to give precise reasons and documentary evidence for why a particular description or explanation of events is offered over others. What *unites* history with fiction is its dependence on narrative discourse and creative synthesis in order that events have meaning and purpose. As with traditional fiction, history seeks both closure and completeness but can attain them only through selection and by applying the formal beginning-middle-end structure of narrative—which then implies "discovering" such teleologies in the events of the past. As we learned from MacIntyre, it is often the story within which events are framed that first gives them their importance.[88]

This interweaving of history and fiction is taken up in an interesting way by Ricoeur in the third volume of his *Time and Narrative,* and it will be pertinent to look at some of his conclusions here. Ricoeur's hermeneutical project has always been concerned with the pervasiveness of the "seeing as" structure in human experience and, concomitant with this, the necessary mediatory role of imagination as it generates adequate representative figures for the past. It is Ricoeur's thesis that "seeing as" and productive imagination are common to both history and fiction such that history is seen to be "quasi-fictive" and fiction "quasi-historical" (3:190f). These two genres of narrative are shown to be mutually dependent and together serve the important role, at the reception stage, of refiguring our experience in its temporal dimensions.[89]

History relies on imagination for its attempt at a reenactment (Collingwood's term) of the past, a reenactment that aims at making the otherness of the past less foreign: "It is always through some transfer from Same to Other, in empathy and imagination, that the Other that is foreign to me is brought closer" (3:184). The other must be brought into some significant relation to my present, must be reconstructed (configured) within a life context (social, cultural, etc.) that can be understood by extension from my own). In the last resort, the historian presents the past such that one gains some sense of actually being there, albeit in the mode of the "as if" (3:185). To aid in obtaining this type of fulfillment, historical imagination also borrows from cultural traditions various genres and rhetorical devices of literary emplotment: tragedy, comedy, romance, irony, analogy, and the like. The employment of such devices, sometimes unconsciously, often follows from the motivation and interests that serve to isolate the historian's field of investigation; it is, for example, understandable that an account of the Holocaust will take on the rhetoric of tragedy.

The above factors explain why many great works of historical writing could be read as though they were novels. On the other hand, however, it is easy to see why a novel such as Tolstoy's *War and Peace* could be read as history. In fact, the traditional fictive novel, maintains Ricoeur, usually depicts events and states of affairs in a way that makes them seem plausible or possible given our prior knowledge of the world. This is, of course, a point stressed long ago by Aristotle in his *Poetics*. Ricoeur, however, enriches this claim by adding that what is encountered in the fictional work can be read as a "quasi-past," in this case the past of the narrative voice: "Fictional narrative is quasi-historical to the extent that the unreal events that it relates are past facts for the narrative voice that addresses itself to the reader" (3:190). Thus, through a certain willing suspension of disbelief, we read the fictional work "as if" it were a recounting of an actual past. This, says Ricoeur, is part of the pact we enter into with the author when reading such works. A major value of the fictional, to return to Aristotle, is to disclose possibilities in the real past which, to follow Ricoeur, aid in the imaginative refiguring of the reader's own world. In this regard, one has only to think of the way stories and myths enter into the sense a community has of its own historical identity.

Ricoeur's work clearly offers a firm basis for further considerations of the interpenetration of history and fiction and of their mutual effect in forming our own sense of the temporality and historicality of experience. This interweaving has, especially in the latter half of the twentieth century, been put through interesting and provocative variations in the works of various postmodern or metafictional novelists, often with a more theoretical aim of problematizing the entire history-fiction dichotomy. Salman Rushdie's *Midnight's Children,* for example, explicitly weaves together historical fact and fiction into a narrative that appears self-consciously aware of its fictive transgressions while being sure of its possible effect in refiguring our sense of the past.

One might well claim, in light of our above considerations of history and narrative, that the problem with conceiving historical discourse (and our own biographical self-narrations) along narrative lines is that (1) this does not satisfy our more positivist longing for empirical exactitude and disinterestedness, and (2) it opens the gates to potential abuse: to constructing a past that suits, say, one's ideological purposes. This latter point indicates a potential disfiguring and not merely refiguring effect of both historical and fictive narratives.

In response to the first of these objections, I shall only say here that empirical exactitude makes for boring history, history without life's drama.[90] History without interpretative narrative emplotment, which gives meaning to the events related, would in fact be an impoverished account of human experience and social transactions, especially if we are correct in granting such transactions a quasi-narrative status in the first instance. Similarly, empirical exactitude applies only to dates, places, and documented evidence. The more global meaning of these events and reports is developed in the story, which is told after the fact and which cannot be said to simply correspond to any of "the facts."

Thus, one does not report an already constituted meaning of the past; rather, one seeks a narrative that synthesizes the various threads of the past into a coherent, meaningful, and plausible account. Such plausibility may depend on factors (e.g., future events) not at all present to the actors of the events being considered. Furthermore, disinterestedness may be an ideal here, but it is hardly a practical one from a hermeneutic point of view.[91] The positivist's claim applies primarily to the necessary empirical analyses that precede the actual writing of history.

The second objection, ideological abuse, is one that continually threatens any discourse concerning a cultural study of man. As human beings we are quite simply prey to fallibility, to self-deception, and to self-edifying discourse; we have no neutral vantage point from which to make final judgments. Hayden White adds a new and valuable slant to this ideological component of history when he says:

> it may be observed that if historians were to recognize the fictive element in their narratives, this would not mean the degradation of historiography to

> the status of ideology or propaganda. In fact, this recognition would serve as a potential antidote to the tendency of historians to become captive of ideological preconceptions which they do not recognize as such but honour as the "correct" perception of "the way things *really* are."[92]

The legitimization of one narrative over another is often due not to its correspondence to "the way things really are" but to its pragmatic and comprehensive nature. Is it edifying, without being narcissistic or egotistic? Does it make sense of what we otherwise know? Is it useful in furthering other and interesting interpretations? It would seem that a primary way to overcome, at least in part, the ideological use of language is to open ourselves to alternative viewpoints and world views, and to alternate interpretations. Anthropological studies and the reading of literature, for example, especially serve in this regard to broaden our knowledge of human society and sharpen our critical capacities with respect to restrictive and dogmatic narratives. A great deal could be said concerning this problem of legitimation, for it has far-reaching social and political ramifications; here I can only point the reader to the various works of Jurgen Habermas as an introduction and working out of some of these important questions.

We have seen that the adequacy of our self-narrations is not a matter of carrying over into language what we already know of ourselves, but is instead a matter of a creative adequation that first generates an explicit sense from our otherwise mute (though significant) prenarrative experience. Imaginative elaboration and potential distortion cannot be exorcised from this latter process. Authenticity, after all, is not the mere recounting of one's past but, as Heidegger has said, also the projection of one's possibilities. And besides, the meaning or story of the past, provided we are not hard-core objectivists, continues developing until that life of which it is a constitutive part itself draws to a conclusion.

The Cogito

> From my childhood I lived in a world of books. . . .
>
> Descartes
> *Discourse on Method*[93]

Before bringing together the results of our investigation of the self, it is appropriate to return at this point to a brief examination of the Cartesian cogito, if only because Descartes inaugurated much of what I am arguing against. In earlier chapters certain problems surrounding the Cartesian cogito were noted, and we are now in a position to pursue these issues more thoroughly. My primary concern will be to bring out, in accordance with our recent investigations, the consequences of the spoken quality of the cogito. In Descartes's texts it is this spoken quality that is overlooked.

What in particular the Cartesian philosophy instigated was a shift toward an indubitably given subject that could itself become the ground for a more scientific, primarily epistemological philosophy. The Cartesian moment of self-certainty is the guarantor of truth and the overcoming of both relativism and scepticism. This turn toward the subject as what is immediately accessible had the correlative function of relegating objects to the status of mediated, secondary phenomena:

> although the things which I sense and which I imagine are perhaps nothing at all apart from me, I am nevertheless sure that those modes of thought which I call sensations and imaginations, only just as far as they are modes of thought, reside and are found with certainty in myself. (Med. III, p. 91)

The orientation that Descartes gave philosophy provided the impetus for the unfolding of the Kantian system and continued its effect at least up to Hegel.

There are two problems (though in essence they are one) that arise from the Cartesian position; both are metaphysical. In dispossessing objectivity of a reality other than that of a *cogitatum,* philosophy became burdened with the problem of accessing the "things in themselves." A decisive split results between spirit and nature (*res cogitans* and *res extensa*).[94] The second problem concerns the other pole of the cogito—not the status of what thought intends but the I or ego that intends it, that is cognizant of it. If that which is intended has determinations but is ontologically dubitable, the I (ego) has no determinations but is indubitable.

We might wish to see thoughts (*cogitata*) as determinations of this ego, but they are really only occasions for its apperception. The ego is a *res,* a something that thinks, a *subjectum* whose thought is immediately given to itself. The *cogitata* may be predicated of the ego (as its acts) but they are still nevertheless known by it as objects. That Descartes isolates both I and mind from its acts is clear from the following statement: "Nor can the faculties of willing, perceiving, understanding, and so forth be called parts of the mind, for it is the same mind which wills, perceives, and understands" (Med. VI, p. 139). The mind thus has ontological priority over its own acts.

The ego is, for Descartes, not itself an object but a transcendence. As Kant was later to say, the "I think" must be capable of accompanying all of my representations, but it is not itself a representation.[95] The essence of the Cartesian subject lies in this moment of self-consciousness, this presence to its representations. However, the I or ego itself appears to be contentless and fundamentally ahistorical, for content and change will properly pertain only to the temporal and spatial representations that the ego has. The ego is thus posited as the ontological ground for the very possibility of both history and representation. Descartes's I in fact remains anonymous unless we turn back to the *cogitata* themselves, and also to their historical context and their production.[96]

For all its absoluteness the Cartesian cogito is fraught with frailties. Consider dreams. Can I always actualize the "I think" during dreams? Am "I," in fact, the dreamer? As is known, Descartes does not clearly address this problem. In saying that even if what I take to be my waking life is nothing but a dream, I nevertheless cannot doubt that I am, Descartes is referring to the "I" that exists even within deception, but not to what we properly call dreams. Similarly, there are also psychological cases such as split personality, where we find two or more possible and even mutually exclusive cogitos!

What needs to be brought out in the Cartesian philosophy is the status of the cogito as language event. As Descartes writes, "*I am, I exist,* is necessarily true every time that I pronounce it or conceive it in my mind" (Med. II, p. 82). This pronouncing seems to us all-important, for it is difficult to see how conception can be achieved outside this pronunciation (be it aloud or to oneself). Descartes does not come back to pronunciation other than to say:

> I am, I exist—that is certain; but for how long do I exist? For as long as I think; for it might perhaps happen, if I totally ceased thinking, that I would at the same time completely cease to be. (Med. II, p. 84)

This statement should remind us of Helen Keller's observations; it points to the fact that we can take Descartes's statement more literally than he perhaps intended. For Descartes, however, *res cogitans* still harbors traits from scholastic ontology, especially unity and indestructibility.

But who or what is the "I"? Is it solely an impersonal transcendental ego, or is it the person we call Descartes? In the text we clearly have a sense of both meanings, though they are not explicitly separated. One of the "egos" clearly has a history, and Descartes in fact offers an autobiographical account of himself in the opening sections of the *Discourse on Method.* Here the I is not the bloodless and anonymous epistemically foundational subject; and is this I not found throughout the *Meditations* as the subject who actually inquires after itself, the narrator? It is this latter I—let us call it Descartes—whose history leads itself to pose the question of certainty in a fight against scepticism. It is Descartes who has perceived, doubted, and dreamed, and it is he therefore who embodies the context within which radical doubt may arise. The I of the cogito is located ontologically outside the narrative of Descartes's systematic meditations and yet is temporally a product of it, parasitic on it. As Merleau-Ponty remarks, "The question is how subjectivity can be both dependent yet irremovable."[97]

As in the case of Kant, the Cartesian "I think" is a manifestation of the spontaneity of the transcendental ego, the sheer mineness (and hence unity) of experience. But this I is as empty as the bare form of temporality. It is only, and here we refer back to Husserl, in the "unity of a history" that individual persons are manifest, and it is here that the *Discourse on Method* in fact begins; cogitos come later. An important question to ask at this point concerns the explanatory value of the I disclosed in the cogito. Can the unity or synthesizing powers it exemplifies be demonstrated? Is it in fact anything more than a mode of address? In sum, what does the "I" refer to, what does it designate?

The cogito can be said to be to the extent that I pronounce it, but it is more than this, for I may be just blindly repeating Descartes's phrase, much as a child repeats its name without knowing the significance accruing to it. The I must become *my* I; it must be indubitable in my own intuition, my own experience. The cogito must be the expression of my own being, a reenactment of the ontological moment of self-certainty. As Merleau-Ponty has written, "The *cogito* at which we arrive by reading Descartes is . . . a spoken *cogito,* put into words and understood in words. . . ."[98] Thus the "I" is not before the words, just as I never discover myself at the origin of the words I say. The cogito must be spoken, for it is only in the spontaneous upsurge of language and expression that I find myself.[99] I then acquiesce to the logic of the expression, think myself into being as it were. I become the "I" spoken of. But this "I" is nothing more than an index of the person who speaks it, qua speaker: the speaking being.

The self-referentiality of the "I," as has already been suggested, lies initially not in a prelinguistic or transcendental subject but in the auto-affection of speaking-hearing. This phenomenon is certainly a relation of oneself to oneself, but, unlike the relation touching-touched, language also designates the subject of this relation by the personal pronoun. One does not simply hear; one also names oneself with the universal subject "I." Again, the reification of this universal subject seems to me an adequate explanation of the problematic transcendental ego and, as was previously stressed, this arises from a forgetfulness of the constitutive power of speaking; one believes that saying "I" relates back to something other than a speaking subject at the moment of speaking. (Many of the problems surrounding this speaking subject have already been investigated in earlier sections, and will not be repeated here.) The iterability of the cogito, the ability we have continually to repeat or reactivate it, reinforces our belief in the transtemporal unity of the ego and creates the illusion of having a stable identity (a self) throughout the flux of empirical differences.

Historically, the idealist metaphysics of the subject began to be undermined shortly after Hegel, with the rise of dialectical materialism coming out of Feuerbach and receiving its definitive form in Marx. A parallel rejection of the Cartesian standpoint occurs in nineteenth-century positivism. But it was not until the twentieth century that language was clearly perceived as playing a central role in this deconstruction. Heidegger's replacement of the subject-object dichotomy (along with all its metaphysical baggage) with the notion of *Dasein* as being-in-the-world, for example, inaugurated a new era in European philosophy by resituating the subject inextricably within both a world and a language.

The Semiotic Subject

It is time to draw together the various threads of the previous sections into a model of the human subject that respects its situatedness in language and signification. I will call this subject the *semiotic subject*. The label *semiotic* is preferable to any derivation from the word *language* since, while remaining within the realm of signification, its extension is broader. Though language is perhaps the most important signifying system, it is clear, to take one example, that art in its various nonlinguistic forms can also express the subject.[100]

A person is a being of semiosis, a living body of gestures and articulations that exists in extensive interaction with other acting bodies and the products of semiosis—speech, texts, art works, and meaningful action generally. The development of the person will depend on a reflective grasp of, and habitual participation in, this network of social communication and praxis. The human subject must thus be situated within the structures that sustain it rather than posited as transcendent to them; it must be implicated in the production of such structures but need not be taken as foundational.

I have tried to show how the subject, in losing its autonomy, is both decentered and split, coming to itself across the divide demanded by expression, not in the immediacy of self-transparent intuition. While I have disparaged authorial intention, I have nevertheless sought to retain the notion of intention, of *vouloir dire,* because it establishes the speaking subject's essential "wanting to be"—regardless of the degree to which this is determined beforehand by one's habitus. Though structuralism, for example, has gone a long way toward eradicating the causal efficacy of the subject by reducing it to a puppet of structural systems, it is clear that such an impersonal approach is of limited applicability.

There is, as we saw earlier, a spontaneity of the subject that has to do with the way it gradually appropriates and refigures its social world. This is not to say, however, that the subject can be extracted from this network of processes and significations and still retain an identity as subject, for this spontaneity remains one with the malleability of the social structures themselves. Social structures undoubtedly determine individual possibilities (as is the case for language and history, to which we are subjected); they do so, however, only because, on the other side of the coin, the individual has those possibilities open to it. Such possibilities are what ground the notion of intention. In fact, a more favorable interpretation of structuralism would be to see it not as committing one to the rejection of the subject (and subjectivity) but simply as refusing to separate the subject from the social order, thereby rejecting the notion of a free or autonomous foundational subject. In talking only of structures, structuralism will therefore imply subjects to which these pertain, for the two cannot, in the end, be separated.[101] Whether we turn to anthropology or linguistics it is obvious that subjects are always implied; the problem to be dealt with is the function and place of these subjects.[102]

This question of the efficacy and value of the subject ties directly into the question of authorship (and ultimately into authority). It is fairly common, especially in literary circles, to hear of the "death of the author," the notion that one should examine texts on their own merit rather than viewing them as mirrors of a constituting consciousness. The same argument would hold for speech. There is much that we can agree with in this stance, but it will be useful to consider exactly where this position leaves us with regard to the speaking subject. We shall refer to both Roland Barthes and Michel Foucault on this issue.

Writing, says Barthes, "can no longer designate an operation of recording, notation, representation, 'depiction' (as the Classics would say)", for the "scriptor" does not exist outside the scene of writing.[103] The author must "die" for the text to begin its own life, a life without final closure, without a final signified content. The text's future lies in the hands of its readers. But while the psychophysical author (the person) is left behind, what we have called a subject of speech remains:

> Linguistically, the author is never more than the instance writing, just as *I* is nothing more than the instance saying *I*: language knows a "subject," not a "person," and this subject, empty outside the enunciation which defines it, suffices to make the language "hold together," suffices, that is to say, to exhaust it. (IMT, p. 145)

Parallel to the way Barthes moves from author to scriptor, we must note here a similar move from the speaking subject to the linguistic subject. Just as it may seem banal or even tautological to talk only of a scriptor in the context of writing, so it may also appear obvious that in a purely linguistic context we can only talk of subjects of enunciations and not flesh and blood persons; in a text there are only signified subjects, subjects of speech. This situation need not, however, deny the reality of authors or persons insofar as it restricts its claim to the linguistic.

Barthes's linguistic "I" is nothing other than the subject of speech we isolated in Benveniste, an "I" that is usually taken to denote a speaking subject. Barthes's point is that the "I" of a literary text, be it a character or narrator, cannot be innocently ascribed to a "real author" (a phrase we will use for the flesh and blood author). The real author is left behind once the text goes public. Nevertheless, the causal efficacy of this author is attested to in Barthes's remark: "His only power is to mix writings, to counter the ones with the others. . . ." (IMT, p. 146). The author is thus a confluence of intertextuality. He or she cannot escape linguisticality and intertextuality even on the expressive plane:

> Did he wish to *express himself,* he ought at least to know that the inner "thing" he thinks to "translate" is itself only a ready-formed dictionary, its words only explainable through other words, and so on indefinitely. . . . (IMT, p. 146)

Thus, beneath the written (and spoken) words there are only more words, words that are the life of the author, words that even replace passions and feelings. Barthes writes:

> Succeeding the Author, the scriptor no longer bears within him the passions, humours, feelings, impressions, but rather this immense dictionary from which he draws a writing that can know no halt: life never does more than imitate the book. . . ." (IMT, p. 147)

This rejection of authorial intention as being anything other than a potential expression is something we should now be familiar with. The real author has no access to thoughts other than those he himself expresses, in language or otherwise.

We have already seen that even passions and feelings are largely inseparable from interpretation and that the so-called neutral impressions of perception are themselves framed by a certain world view which cuts out and defines elements in the perceptual field. Emotions and passions are best seen as a motivation or impetus for expression and action within the symbolic and cultural spheres.[104] The development of our expressive capacity goes hand in hand with the broadening of affective experience. It is in this respect that life can be viewed as imitating literature (or some other signifying medium such as song or film), for literature provides us with a rich vocabulary for articulating, and thus interpreting, experience in ways previously unsuspected.

But whereas language may only "know" a subject, the reader to whom the text is destined also knows persons—the embodied speaking subject. The body is, as we saw earlier, both the site of narration and the site of ascription or predication for utterances. (A parallel can be made for action generally, in terms, say, of a "site of production" and a "site of responsibility"; this would yield an agent.) This ascription is clear for face to face dialogue, but it also pertains to literature. One generally assumes fictional utterances to be the product of a (fictional) speaking spatiotemporally located human body (exempting some science fiction). To put this another way, we know that texts imply authors—authors who are usually named at the beginning of the text. It is to this named or supposed author that the text is attributed, and with this attribution goes a degree of responsibility for that text. This is not to deny, however, that the author is in turn defined in and through the text. We would also not want to deny that a psychological reading can yield insights into the character or personality of the *real* author, though the proof of such claims would presumably have to be corroborated by something other than the text itself if that text is not to fool us into misguided assumptions.

Barthes explicitly separates, somewhat boldly, the authorial function of texts from that of the persons who write them. Even his autobiography, *Roland Barthes,* is prefaced by the statement: "It must be considered as if spoken by a character in a novel."[105] While accepting the general framework of this separation of author-writer, we nevertheless wish to propose a closer link between the two categories, for the human subject is a semiotic subject that must become its own author in order to define itself. As Foucault has said in his influential essay "What Is an Author,"

> the subject should not be entirely abandoned. It should be reconsidered, not to restore the theme of an originating subject, but to seize its functions, its intervention in discourse, and its systems of dependencies.[106]

The path we have been pursuing throughout this work is one that describes just these dependencies of the subject on language and discourse. We can only definitively separate the subject from discourse at the expense of that subject, for the subject is an implicate of its discourse. Foucault's remark points to a needed rehabilitation or reinscription of this subject into the realm of signification (literary or otherwise). The "author function," as Foucault says, is one of the forms in which the subject is manifest, though not necessarily in a one-to-one relation.[107] Texts, like speeches and even casual discussions, have social conditions and expectations attached to them. Each mode of signification may have its particular restraints and freedoms. Each may set up a different subject as its implied origin. Consider, for example, the difference between a poem, a scientific manual, and a charter of rights. Even from the point of view of the speaker, there are different personae, different roles to be assumed, in these different discourses.

Is there a central organizing "I" behind these various roles? Only if we should choose or be led to *believe* so: if we believe that the "true me," for example, appears under such and such conditions. Later, of course, we may come to see the folly of this belief, or revise it in light of certain experiences or theories. Either way, however, it is not that we behave contradictorily in our lives, for this is still to postulate a subject at the center of things that is enduring and is able to contradict itself. It is rather the case that social reality demands, during our life (even during a single day), that we be different, diverse, that we assume various guises or roles *as our own.* As Barthes remarks,

> This is why, when we speak today of a divided subject . . . it is a *diffraction* which is intended, a dispersion of energy in which there remains neither a central core nor a structure of meaning: I am not contradictory, I am dispersed.[108]

Even the body can be seen as plural, dispersed among a repertoire of roles such as the sensual, digestive, athletic, sick, emotive, mimetic, gestural, and so on.[109]

Given this diversity, the possibility of unity for the subject can only arise through two primary channels: routine activity at the level of praxis and acts of self-narration. In the first case, identity is a matter of repetition, of having a schedule that one repeats daily, weekly, etc. Because this type of identity is largely unconscious, it will take something like sickness to bring our implicit dependence on it to the foreground. My earlier discussion of habitus has much to do with this form of identity. The second option, self-narration, is the properly conscious form of human identity. Only here is the implicit order (or disorder) and structure of our lives taken up into conscious understanding. It is also in narration that we seek to tie together the more disparate strands of our lives, of our history.

I would like now to present a model of the human subject, the semiotic subject, that respects Barthes's observations while fulfilling Foucault's demand for a resituated subject. This model, which I employed in earlier sections of this book, is based on a tripartite division of the subject: the *speaking subject* or material agent of discourse, the *subject of speech* or purely linguistic subject of the discourse (designated by personal pronouns and other deictical indications), and the *spoken subject* or subject produced through or by the discourse as a result of its effect on a reader-listener.[110]

Thus, for example, in the case of self-narration, of the past, the speaking subject is myself qua language user and "repository of images" (and hence conditioned and restricted by that language, by tradition, and by past experience). This narrative then sets up a subject of speech, the character signified by the pronoun *I* and involved in a certain narrated life situation. What then makes this narrative personally historical or autobiographical is that I correlatively become the spoken subject of the narrative—just as a spectator might identify with some character in a play or film. Of course this third stage might be thwarted; the identification might not occur or it may occur when the subject of speech is a fabrication or lie with no direct relation to one's actual memories or prior narratives.

A diagram may help us see the relations between the three subjects more clearly.

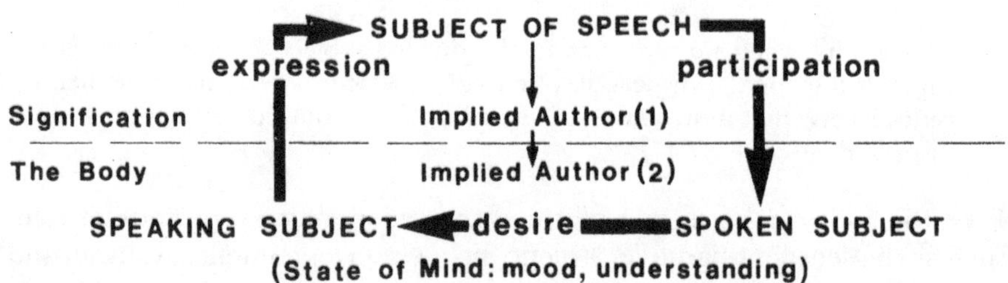

The diagram shows two primary realms: signification and body. Through expression the embodied speaking subject enters the realm of signification. The utterance, if it is autobiographical, relates back to the embodied subject in two ways: by *implication* and by *participation*. The first generally occurs on the part of an addressee or receiver. If I write a letter to a friend, for example, I become for the reader the implied author (2) of the correspondence. If the letter were anonymous the exact site of ascription for the implied author could be lacking; this would lead to implied author (1). A more common academic use of implied author (1) is the literary one, where a text is said to set up an implied author that cannot be naively identified with the real author. We tend to attribute, in one way or another, almost all texts to an implied author.[111] One may even adopt the receiver standpoint to one's own utterances.

By participation is meant the various forms of identification that the embodied subject has in relation to an utterance and its subject of speech (a relation that may also be seen as one of mimesis, a term that is central is Ricoeur's more recent work[112]). Very often the immediacy of listening to speaking carries one in an unbroken and unreflective reciprocity forward into further articulations. Here there can be immediate identification with the subject of speech. But such immediacy can break down.

When narrating one's past it is often the case that first attempts are unsatisfactory: the recollections are seen as too sketchy or perhaps as fabrications; there is a rejection of the implied subject (of speech) as being or properly representing oneself. This rejection of one's own narrative is, as we have seen, central to the theory grounding psychoanalysis. Another revealing example of participation occurs in acts of rage (or drunkenness) where one's emotions cause one to say things that at the time one positively identifies with, and which later seem exorbitant and excessive. The act of participation can also take us out of ourselves. In reading a novel a certain relinquishment of self[113] occurs that is necessary for us to participate in the values, characters, and action of the drama. The sympathy we feel for a certain character, say, is a form of this participation in narratives that are not of our own making.[114]

The spoken subject that participation results in is particularly evident in cinema. Consider how we often, on the visual level, identify with the camera's perspective, especially if the shot is taken from approximately head height. Again, consider how we can walk out of an adventure film feeling somewhat inspired by the hero. In literary criticism this manipulation of the viewing-reading subject is recognized as an essential function of texts. Texts set up not only an implied author but also an implied reader. In a text, the presenting of material in a certain way may not only place restraints on the reader but also set up certain expectations and biases in the reader.[115]

The embodied subject can be characterized in a general way, following Heidegger, as being in a certain state of mind with its moods and degrees and modes of understanding.[116] These general characteristics are what provide the impetus and background for expression, much as unexpressed emotions serve such an impetus in Taylor's analysis, and they are what develop and change in acts of participation.[117] I have labeled the relation between the spoken subject and the speaking subject as *desire,* for this seems to capture the impetus that changing states have for the subject. Earlier I had occasion to define subjectivity as being the possibility of expression. Here we see, in more detail, the dynamics of this more or less continuous state of the subject.

For structuralism (and Barthes in his earlier structural phase), semiotics, and narrative theory (as applied to literature), it is the subject of speech that has been especially emphasized. Indeed, it is here that the stories we tell of ourselves appear in the public arena, and hence where the linguistic subject is constituted. But rather than leave this subject of speech floating in linguistic space, which is the sense one gets from Barthes, the above model attempts to integrate the body back into the equation, not of course as the positivist material body of science but as the speaking-feeling embodied subject (the person). Earlier I talked of the body as both the *site of narration* (the speaking subject) and *site of ascription* (implied author (2)) for the subject; it is here that our commonsense notions of ourselves as embodied subjects are satisfied.

What the above model of the semiotic subject seeks to emphasize is the division of the subject into different moments with no central and organizing core. Subjectivity is itself blind without mediation through the realm of signification, but signification is not a neutral mirroring process. Subjectivity, as a form of *vouloir dire* (a wanting to say, to be, to do), is manifest as the speaking embodied subject that seeks to carry over into expression the implicit truth of itself (its implicit history or story).[118] This expression is a *creative adequation* to what is only schematically given in a quasi-narrative form. The "I" then exists in its communicable form as the subject of speech. Already there is a split here between the speaking subject (what Roman Jakobson called the "subject of the enunciation") and the subject of speech (the "subject of the enounced").[119]

In self-narration the final stage of the semiotic subject is identification with and appropriation of this linguistic subject through the reading-listening process. A split or noncoincidence in the subject is also apparent here due to the interpretive nature of this participation. One may not, for example, accept the expression as an adequate representative of oneself, which may cause the cycle to continue again. This cycle of ever new signification and appropriation is, of course, none other than the dynamic framework within which personal development takes place.[120] To return to Charles Taylor: man "cannot be understood simply as an object among objects, for his life incorporates an interpretation, an expression of what cannot exist unexpressed, because the self that is to be interpreted is essentially that of a being who self-interprets."[121]

IV

CONCLUSION

> It is no longer possible to think in our day other than in the void left by man's disappearance. For this void does not create a deficiency; it does not constitute a lacuna that must be filled. It is nothing more, and nothing less, than the unfolding of a space in which it is once more possible to think.
>
> Michel Foucault
> *The Order of Things*

What we have attempted here is to move behind the scenes of the human drama to discover how our role-playing is enacted, for if one thing is to be concluded from this study it is that human subjects develop (and inherit) the identity of a character in the gradually unfolding narrative that is lived time. This does not imply, however, that we act our parts with blind necessity, for the script is not entirely prewritten; only certain backdrops are preset. As in a first-person narration, we interrupt the ongoing drama with retrospective assessments and refigurations and are not, therefore, completely engulfed in our roles.[1] It is as such a narrator that we make sense of our lives, delineate the character(s) that we are and have been. But, as should now be clear, such seeming self-reflectivity is not that of a pregiven self simply musing over its past and future. Narration is not a gratuitous act as far as the self is concerned.

Self-narration, I have argued, is what first raises our temporal existence out of the closets of memorial traces and routine and unthematic activity, constituting thereby a self as its implied subject. This self is, then, the implied subject of a narrated history. Stated another way, in order to be we must be *as* something or someone, and this someone that we take ourselves to be is the character delineated in our personal narratives.[2] The unity of the self, where such a unity exists, is exhibited as an identity in difference, which is all a temporal character can be.

In his important texts on the literary work of art, Roman Ingarden speaks of what he calls the "idea" of a work, the more or less comprehensive unity we carry away with us when our reading has made us sufficiently familiar with the text.[3] It is this "idea" which allows us to classify the work, as a whole, as of a certain type and as gravitating around a certain problematic and certain values. This notion of "idea" can be seen to apply equally well to the lives of persons, for no matter how diverse a life may be there tends always to exist, upon reflection, that unity of a *Geschichte* of which Husserl spoke in his *Cartesian Meditations*. Temporal existence is such that prior chapters of our life inform and determine, to a greater or lesser degree, later ones. Not that this "idea" fully determines the closure of a life, for we well know that a text has many possible endings, many changes of fortune. We are not dealing here with a metaphysical predestination but rather with a transtemporal kernel of meaning, what Merleau-Ponty termed "style," which satisfies what appears to be our inherent need for understanding, coherence, and unity. As with a novel, this identity need never be settled and final, for the prenarrative out of which it arises need never have a definitive interpretation.[4]

This "idea" (or identity) has the attraction of answering to the perennial question we ask of our own identity, our own reality, and its power over us results in the sedimenting of our identity into a relatively unchanging self-conception. What seems truly unchanging, however, is not so much the content of this identity, for we often do not notice the significant changes time effects, but rather the need for and belief in such an identity, which is correlated to our desire to be. Psychologists have long attested to the fact that the mental health and sanity of the individual requires something more than mere existing and the satisfying of primary bodily needs, for beyond these is required the sense of being *as* someone that I mentioned above.

I have argued that behind the scenes we do not find some form of transcendental ego or omniscient narrator serving as stage director but rather a certain form of activity whereby selves make their appearance as characters. This activity is precisely language usage and expression, particularly the employment of personal pronouns and self-referential narrative structures. The self is thus not a prelinguistic given for whom language is just a tool but is an implicate of language usage. Again, language is not the instrument of an "inner self" (to which we might grant autonomy, free will, and the like) but is one of the body's acquired habitualities, a behavior that becomes as spontaneous and ordered as, say, perceiving. However, language usage, unlike breathing or walking, is a highly social phenomenon, undergirding as it does the whole cultural sphere.

It is in this "intersubjective"—though perhaps one should say with Merleau-Ponty "intercorporeal"—social realm that language functions. Speech does not arise out of a particular ego's intention to speak but is called forth by a social situation, much like many of our other social acts.

Speech is similarly not prefigured in an interiority and then sent forth like the "winged words" of Homer, for even in interior monologue it is not "I" who speaks (except in a retrospective and derivative sense). When we are in the heat of conversation it is particularly evident that what "I" say is not at all prefigured in consciousness but is a spontaneous and bodily response to the speech situation. As Merleau-Ponty wrote, "Neither the word nor the meaning of the word is in fact *constituted* by consciousness."[5] Speech, which should not be seen in this respect as essentially different from other bodily acts, should thus be understood in its overall gestalt, which may or may not include what is commonly called "conscious intentions."

I have also argued ("Signs of Derrida") that there is a good case to be made for developing a theory of meaning and ideality that takes as its basis the material signifier and its iterability and eschews appeal to transcendental signifieds, or what has also been called in the history of philosophy "intelligible essences." Though I cannot here work out the details, what must be addressed in such a position are the various ways in which meaning is generated in associative relations. Meaning is not only a matter of a signifier's difference from other signifying units; it is especially a product of temporal and tropical relations and transformations, e.g., contiguity and juxtaposition, sequence, identity and difference, metonymy and synecdoche, metaphor, and so on. One problem we mistakenly introduce into the consideration of language (as in considering the ego) is to see it as somehow different from everything else, as outside "nature" and capable of reflecting it.

What obscures the above view is a persistent tendency to dematerialize language, to find in it a "spiritual essence" that must be present at its inception.[6] As previously noted, one commonly insists on an "I" that speaks and on a meaning for which language is merely the vehicle. Such a position generates many of the problems that have plagued both philosophy of language and philosophy of mind for centuries. The pronoun *I*, I have argued, simply does not have the independent referential "object" or "substance" often attributed to it, be this soul, mind, or self. "I," as Benveniste has said, designates the speaker of the utterance containing "I"; it designates the site of narration and, in the last resort, the person as an amalgam of self and body. I defined person as the result of ascribing selfhood (in an act of implicit or explicit predication) to the site of narration, the body. The person is thus (though this is not an exhaustive definition) an embodied self. In other words, the body must be seen as the enduring locus to which a life history accrues, and hence to which the character of that history is indissolubly associated.

It should be clear that the traditional mind-body problem receives a very specific treatment in what I have so far claimed. Put in its most striking form, there is no such thing or entity as mind (traditionally conceived; a *res cogitans*) and therefore no obvious problem concerning the relation of mind to body. But of course this answer is too cursory and requires some expansion and clarification.

What I have attempted to undermine in this work is the need for positing a self or mental substance as an underlying cause of our linguistic or other expressions. The self is essentially a meaning construct deriving from language and conversation generally, where language must be seen as essentially "material," that is, as an extension of the sphere of activity of the human body. On the other hand, the human body is alive with expression, with signification. Such a body of gestures we call a *person.* It would be artificial (or at best hypothetical) to introduce into this unity a strict substantial division of body and mind, or body and self. Accordingly, I have defined subjectivity as *the possibility of expression,* but this is not to make of subjectivity some sort of *res cogitans* or thinking power. Subjectivity is nothing but an honorary appellation we give to a being that has the expressive-linguistic capabilities commonly found in persons. It is, in many cases, also predicated because we are able to think and feel without giving explicit external signs of these activities; we thus think of the inmost self as very personal and private, but this does not exempt the self from arising primarily within conversation.[7]

Aristotle argued in *De Anima* that the mind was the *meaning* of the body. Taken in the above way, this is a very appealing and insightful formulation. But as we saw in discussing Husserl and Derrida, we must not conceive of this meaning as independent of the material signifiers (expressions) that give rise to it. Thought, I have maintained, simply does not exist in the absence of language, and meaning is therefore rightly construed as primarily a property of language and not the property of an inner self or nonmaterial mental substance.

The body becomes, through expression, what is called (particularly in existentialism) a lived body, not just an animate organism. This body is in a sense me, is alive with me, both because it is the site of ascription for selfhood and because it is a semiotic body that through its gestures enables and maintains the social realm within which the "I" and "you" function. My investigations prompt me to contend that with a diminution in the semiotic potentiality of the body there will be a correlative diminution in what is called self-consciousness or self-presence.[8] The "I," in other words, requires for its existence the very saying of "I" that is predetermined by participation in the sociolinguistic network. But this is not the blind saying of a machine, a tape recorder, for example; it is rather a saying wherein this "I" becomes thematic in further narrative acts, becomes an object to itself.[9]

Speech, as Merleau-Ponty clearly saw, "*brings about* that concordance between me and myself, and between myself and others. . . ."[10] The "I" appears to break with the body when the dependence of speech on the body (especially on the phonetic) is overlooked and the "I" takes on independent referential status; this is seen especially in the form of "I act." This formulation sets up, for example, the motivating subject that we have already criticized. We have no more need of a motivating subject than a biologist would have of positing a plant soul to explain why plants turn toward the light.

The "I," the self, is an effect of language, and the status and meaning of the self will thus depend on the particular "language game" in which it is invoked and in which it comes into play. But this does not make the self superfluous; it only problematizes it. Who or what the self (and ultimately the person) can be is a result of the semiotic and discursive practices and techniques within which the speaking subject functions. The place of the subject just one century ago differs considerably from that of the subject in the modern industrial and technological era. To take just one example: in the field of artificial intelligence it is no longer just a matter of mapping computational models onto thought and brain characteristics; what we are seeing is a situation in which the very language of computer modeling is gradually replacing the other ways of *speaking* about mind. Orwell's insights in *1984* concerning language and thought are not just possibilities; they have been with us all along.

Freedom and autonomy are, on my account, not elements of a pregiven "human essence"; they are instead measures of the prevailing sociolinguistic system and its customs. Freedom relates to the possibilities for self-definition and expression allowed the individual within the system. Similarly, creativity is not so much the exercising of "freedom" as it is the exercising of the possibilities inherent in signifying networks. Because signifiers function in differential relations and not solely by a system of prefigured meanings, it is possible to generate new and often revealing significances by tropic transformations (metaphor, metonymy, and so on).

A repressive society is one in which this expressive potential is consistently restricted or treated as renegade and antisocial. What lies behind social norms and values is very often an image of humanity that appeals to a fixed essence, one in light of which individuals can be classified as either degenerate or healthy, sane or insane, sinful or virtuous. Foucault's historical study of madness, for example, seeks to show how madness is not simply and not always a physical or medical "disorder," but is a changing category (or definition) operative within a certain sociopolitical and economic system and serves that system by making outsiders of those who threaten its "rational" order and power structure.[11]

The present study has not sought explicitly to examine and criticize the actual content of our self-definitions, though I have pointed to a few implications. I have, instead, restricted myself to a primarily descriptive examination of the framework within which such definitions arise, the language of self-narration.

From what has been something of a survey of contemporary, particularly

European, thought regarding the scope and function of narrative language to the status of the human subject, a few broad conclusions may be drawn. Of first importance is the situating of the subject within the play of language and social structures. This move has the function of displacing the subject from center stage, even to the point of emphasizing certain discontinuities in the subject's identity. While the subject is viewed from the perspective of the history in which it is implicated, working out the subject's history is an interpretive enterprise that can no longer be seen as free from ideological and psychological distortions. The human subject is a self-interpreting animal that, via narration, is of necessity prey to its own "fictions."

Contemporary trends also reveal a marked rejection of metaphysical thinking. Autonomy, freedom, and identity, for example, are not pregiven or a priori characteristics but must be redefined within the context of the person's appearance within the sociolinguistic arena. I have not said much about religious presuppositions concerning the essence of man, but it should be clear that, from a postmodern perspective, religion is a semiotic system that presumes to articulate that which is beyond language and even beyond the given; here one must have faith or a particular belief in the possibility of transcendental signifieds. There is a tendency in contemporary thought, deriving from structuralism, to treat all such speculative, metaphysical, and utopian thought reductively in terms of the social matrix out of which it arises; this acts as a demystifying, if not deconstructive, enterprise. What still balances this latter tendency is a pragmatic strain that, in effect, gives countenance to what works for furthering human community and personal enrichment.

Having shifted the emphasis away from the self as an inner substantial core of personhood, one need not conclude that the human subject is an ephemera of little significance. The constitution of persons through acts of predication remains the most human of acts, one that is central to our Western thinking and general world view. The status of the subject is not necessarily demeaned because it is seen as the product of a creative act rather than as a pregiven entity to be simply recognized and respected.

NOTES

Introduction

1. Donald Polkinghorne, *Narrative Knowing and the Human Sciences* (Albany, N.Y.: SUNY Press, 1988), is one of the more comprehensive works that have already pursued this narrative itinerary.

2. What I call the "implied subject" has important parallels to what, in literary theory, is called the "implied author." The latter term is employed in two primary and interrelated senses: (1) to designate the status of the author that a text sets up for the reader in and through itself, and (2) to stress that what the text reveals about the "author" cannot be directly identified with the flesh-and-blood author. The term *implied subject* is intended to refer to the subject set up by our utterances, but which, in ordinary language usage at least, does not contain the distance evidenced in point 2. That is, behind our speaking or thinking there is not another (more real) subject or author.

3. I do not intend here a complete overthrow of our beliefs in the existence of selfhood and personal identity, for I do not doubt the importance of these concepts to our lives. The aim is rather to examine the ways in which our experience of selfhood and identity is in fact dependent on language and self-narration.

4. I take the notions of person and personal identity, unlike self and selfhood, to explicitly include embodiment, even if it is a fictional person. Later chapters expand on this distinction.

5. The foundationalist strains in our own age arise especially from the Cartesian stress on an indubitable self that, through the right method, may gain scientific knowledge of its own thoughts *(cogitationes)* and thereby of reality in general. Edmund Husserl continued this project into the twentieth century via his method of transcendental phenomenology. Foundationalism and metaphysics are, in contemporary thought, largely synonymous. This is perhaps understandable if we view metaphysics as *speculative* philosophy. Speculation proceeds by hypothesizing some principle on the basis of which the nature of the phenomenon under investigation can be explained and made understandable. This is fine as long as the principle is not reified into something given, something self-evident; its speculative nature should not be obscured. Speculative philosophy presents only a possibility for thought and understanding; it should not claim certitude. It is because of the hypothetical nature of "first principles" that there is today such a mistrust of metaphysics, for we are always able to ask, "Why this principle and not another?" This question of initial choices soon becomes a discussion of ideological positions and incommensurable world views. The problem one often encounters with metaphysical thought concerns its assumption to have reached a level of fundamental questions where metaphysical choices must be made. Too often, however, we find that other assumptions—about truth, about values, and about the nature of the human subject—have been made and various options excluded prior to the level of fundamental questions, and that this invalidates the metaphysical choices. Metaphysics should not (and perhaps cannot) be ruled out, but it should proceed only after careful consideration and description of human experience and practices.

6. See Alasdair MacIntyre, *After Virtue: A Study in Moral Theory* (Notre Dame,

Ind.: University of Notre Dame Press, 1984): "I inherit from the past of my family, my city, my tribe, my nation, a variety of debts, inheritances, rightful expectations and obligations. These constitute the given of my life, my moral starting point" (p. 220). Carrying this over to the question of narrative, he continues: "the story of my life is always embedded in the story of those communities from which I derive my identity. . . . What I am, therefore, is in key part what I inherit, a specific past that is present to some degree in my present. I find myself part of a history and that is generally to say, . . . whether I recognize it or not, one of the bearers of a tradition" (p. 221).

7. As the psychologist Jerome Bruner has said in *Actual Minds, Possible Worlds* (Cambridge, Mass.: Harvard University Press, 1986), p. 67, "It can never be the case that there is a 'self' independent of one's cultural-historical existence." In this work Bruner develops a position similar to my own, adopting a "transactional" view of self in opposition to an egocentric or private one.

8. Of course, the amnesiac will not necessarily experience a diminished sense of existence. Indeed, in his desperate situation the fact of existence will probably be heightened by his not knowing what, or rather who, he exists *as*. It is the *as* that I take to be the important factor in human selfhood.

9. We can, of course, also become the implied subject of the narrative activity of others, in biographies, for example, or by identifying with a character in a novel. Death relegates us to the permanent status of implied subjects concerning which no new autobiographical utterances are forthcoming.

10. Stephen Crites, "The Narrative Quality of Experience" (*Journal of the American Academy of Religion*, vol. 39, 3, September 1971), pp. 291–305. My own work owes a great debt to this essay, for it served, early on, to bring into clear focus for me the profound relation between narration, experience, and the self. See also Stephen Crites, "Storytime: Recollecting the Past and Projecting the Future," in *Narrative Psychology*, ed. Theodore Sarbin (New York: Praeger, 1986).

11. This is our concession to foundationalism, but it is not enough to ground a theory of truth as correspondence (to the prenarrative level) upon. I will return to this important topic in chap. 3.

12. Vincent Descombes, *Objects of All Sorts: A Philosophical Grammar* (Baltimore: Johns Hopkins University Press, 1987). All quotations are from pp. 4 and 5. It should be pointed out that while Descombes isolates these three trends in contemporary European philosophy, he is not totally in agreement with them as stated in the quotations I refer to. He finds each position ultimately to be inconsistent or obscure with respect to its central tenets.

13. Descombes is referring to Saussure's important lectures *Course in General Linguistics* (New York: McGraw-Hill, 1966).

14. To see these stages as a "development" is to describe the way they were taken up into twentieth-century philosophy. Their actual genesis was fairly simultaneous, especially if we emphasize the pioneering works of Husserl, Dilthey, and Peirce.

15. For a discussion of this issue, see Paul Ricoeur, "The Question of the Subject: The Challenge of Semiology," *The Conflict of Interpretations* (Evanston, Ill.: Northwestern University Press, 1974).

16. Leslie Dewart, *Evolution and Consciousness: The Role of Speech in the Origin and Development of Human Nature* (Toronto: University of Toronto Press, 1989), offers an insightful analysis of human nature that is sympathetic to the Darwinian, or evolutionary, perspective. Dewart nevertheless claims that mere experience undergoes a qualitative change toward consciousness with the advent of speech and that a scientific approach is perniciously reductive if this factor is not adequately addressed.

17. Semiotics, or semiology, deriving from the Greek *semion* (sign), is essentially a science of signs and communication. As such, its range is understandably large.

18. As Roland Barthes has written, following Benveniste, "Man does not exist prior to language, either as a species or as an individual. We never encounter a state where man is separated from language, which he then elaborates in order to 'express' what is happening within him: it is language which teaches the definition of man, not the contrary." *The Rustle of Language,* trans. Richard Howard (New York: Hill and Wang, 1986), p. 13.

19. Cf. Charles Taylor, *Human Agency and Language: Philosophical Papers I* (Cambridge: Cambridge University Press, 1985), p. 7: "As for any hermeneutic explanation, interpretive plausibility is the ultimate criterion." Much of Taylor's introduction to his volume is instructive with respect to the nature of hermeneutic explanation in the human sciences.

1. Time and Memory

1. M. Merleau-Ponty, *Phenomenology of Perception,* trans. Colin Smith (London: Humanities Press, 1962), p. 432.

2. W. James, *The Principles of Psychology* (Cambridge, Mass.: Harvard University Press, 1983), p. 574.

3. See Husserl's 1905–10 lectures collected in *The Phenomenology of Internal Time-Consciousness* (Bloomington: Indiana University Press, 1964) for a thorough discussion of these and related matters.

4. Merleau-Ponty, *Phenomenology of Perception,* p. 69.

5. See H. Bergson, *Matter and Memory,* trans. Nancy Paul and Scott Palmer (New York: Humanities Press, 1970).

6. See Paul Ricoeur, *Time and Narrative,* vol. 1, trans. K. McLaughlin and D. Pellauer (Chicago: University of Chicago Press, 1984), for a thorough and insightful discussion of Augustine's investigation into temporality.

7. Merleau-Ponty, *Phenomenology of Perception,* p. 422.

8. To reiterate a point made in the introduction, I am offering here a descriptive and not a speculative account of the human subject. That human experience should be explained proceeding from a transcendental or founding subject seems to me an unnecessary hypothesis, though one that cannot be definitively refuted. It is my belief that whereas human experience contains a number of relatively abiding characteristics that can be described or otherwise indicated, metaphysical theories concerning how experience got to be as it is are, at least potentially, innumerable.

9. E. Husserl, *Cartesian Meditations: An Introduction to Phenomenology,* trans. Dorian Cairns (The Hague: Martinus Nijhoff, 1970), §37.

10. James, *Principles of Psychology,* p. 322.

11. Husserl, *Cartesian Meditations,* §32.

12. Ibid., §32.

13. Where "ego" refers to a pole of identity rather than to a substantial entity. Consciousness, for Husserl, may be considered from either of its two poles or moments: subject and object. But this is only a theoretical division, for consciousness necessarily consists in an intention on the part of a subject toward an object.

14. Pierre Bourdieu, *Outline of a Theory of Practice,* trans. Richard Nice (New York: Cambridge University Press, 1982), pp. 78, 72.

15. Merleau-Ponty, *Phenomenology of Perception,* p. 22.

16. In *Remembering: A Phenomenological Study* (Bloomington: Indiana University Press, 1987) Edward Casey, following Husserl, makes a similar distinction between

"primary" and "secondary" remembering (see pp. 48–52). Primary remembering, says Casey, is the persistence of the immediate past (retention) in the present moment of consciousness, whereas secondary remembering is the recollection "of experiences that had lapsed from my consciousness after their initial occurrence" (p. 50). This latter form, says Casey, is what, in ordinary parlance, we generally mean by remembering. Casey's work is highly illuminating in its descriptions of the many different ways in which recollection occurs in our daily lives. For a recent consideration of Husserl's lectures on time consciousness, see Ricoeur, *Time and Narrative,* vol. 3 (Chicago: University of Chicago Press, 1988), pt. 4, sec. 1, §2. Ricoeur masterfully reveals both the value and the drawbacks of the phenomenological approach to time (via a confrontation with Kant's analysis in the first critique). While Husserl's descriptions are adequate to certain of our fundamental experiences with temporal objects and particularly with memorial events, they are not adequate to other dimensions of our temporal experience. As a corrective, Ricoeur proceeds to Heidegger, who reoriented the phenomenological analysis of time toward the future and its concomitant, expectation. But more than this, Heidegger deepens the analysis by disclosing a hermeneutical and broader historical dimension. From here, the stage is set for Ricoeur's narratological contribution, which attempts to mediate the aporias that still remain after Heidegger's incomplete *Being and Time.* Narrative will bridge the abyss between lived time and objective, or cosmic, time. "Human time," concludes Ricoeur, "is nothing other than narrated time" (3:102). Our own itinerary will lead us to much the same conclusion as Ricoeur's work, though via a somewhat different route and with a more pointed emphasis on the human subject.

17. J. Locke, *An Essay Concerning Human Understanding* (New York: Dover, 1959), vol. 1, p. 451.

18. Gaston Bachelard, *The Poetics of Space,* trans. M. Jolas (Boston: Beacon Press, 1968). There is, given the interweaving of imagination and memory, good argument for adopting the more Kantian terminology of *reproductive* versus *productive* imagination, thereby subsuming recollection under the more general heading of presentations. However, a systematic inquiry into these matters is not my purpose here. It is hoped that the reader's own experience bears witness to my general distinctions.

19. Locke, *Essay Concerning Human Understanding,* vol. 1, pp. 449, 464. The implication of Locke's view is that substance may change while identity persists. This of course places the onus on memory, the "storehouse of our ideas."

20. Ibid., p. 448.

21. Ibid., pp. 444ff.

22. For Descartes, the "I think" presupposes the "I am," whereas Locke reverses this relation.

23. Quoted in Locke, *An Essay Concerning Human Understanding,* vol. 1, p. 458, n. 1.

24. D. Hume, *A Treatise of Human Nature* (Oxford: Clarendon Press, 1981), p. 252.

25. Ibid., pp. 261–63.

26. Ibid., p. 262.

27. This point relates back to our earlier discussion of images as tokens or representatives of the past. The recollected image of someone we know may well be interpreted in a variety of ways at various times and thus take on significantly different meanings and values. The same phenomenon is found in the case of a photograph (which is, in itself, unchanging) of some acquaintance.

28. James Olney, *Metaphors of Self: The Meaning of Autobiography* (Princeton, N.J.: Princeton University Press, 1981), p. 44.

29. Marcel Proust, "Contre Saint-Beuve," *On Art and Literature, 1896–1919*, trans. Sylvia Townsend Warner (New York: Carroll and Graf, 1984), p. 19.

30. Ibid., p. 17.

31. Ibid., p. 19.

32. M. Proust, *Remembrance of Things Past,* vol. 2, trans. Scott Moncrieff (New York: Random House, 1934), p. 1014.

33. G. Santayana, *Scepticism and Animal Faith* (New York: Dover, 1955), p. 158.

34. Ibid.

35. For Wilhelm Dilthey meaning is always the product of a backward reflection: "The category of meaning designates the relationship, inherent in life, of parts of a life to the whole. The connections are only established by memory, through which we can survey the past. Here meaning takes the form of comprehending life." *Dilthey: Selected Writings,* ed. H. P. Rickman (New York: Cambridge University Press, 1976), p. 235. One can trace the same line of thought to the phenomenological sociology of Alfred Schutz: "Meaning does not lie *in* the experience. Rather, those experiences are meaningful which are grasped reflectively." *The Phenomenology of the Social World* (Evanston, Ill.: Northwestern University Press, 1967), p. 69.

36. Rudolf Bultmann, *New Testament and Mythology and Other Basic Writings,* trans. S. M. Ogden (Philadelphia: Fortress Press, 1984), p. 136.

2. On Narrative

1. F. Nietzsche, *The Will to Power,* trans. W. Kaufmann and R. J. Hollingdale (New York: Vintage Books, 1968), p. 631.

2. Our progress through the various "stages" from childhood to old age is not without its forgetfulness of the aspirations and accomplishments of earlier stages. As Nietzsche has taught us, forgetfulness is a virtue where advancement is concerned.

3. Hannah Arendt, *The Human Condition* (Chicago: University of Chicago Press, 1981), p. 186.

4. MacIntyre, *After Virtue,* p. 217.

5. D. Parfit, *Reasons and Persons* (Oxford: Clarendon Press, 1984).

6. Arendt, *Human Condition,* p. 192. The use of "always" is somewhat strong in Arendt's remark. She presumably means *may* know better.

7. Ibid., p. 179.

8. Kate Hamburger had much to do with promoting this distinction. See *The Logic of Literature,* trans. M. J. Rose (Bloomington: Indiana University Press, 1973).

9. Cf. Peter Brooks, *Reading for the Plot: Design and Intention in Narrative* (New York: Vintage Books, 1985), p. xi: "Plot as I conceive it is the design and intention of narrative, what shapes a story and gives it a certain direction or intent of meaning. We might think of plot as the logic or perhaps the syntax of a certain kind of discourse, one that develops its propositions only through temporal sequence and progression."

10. Cf. ibid. "Narrative is one of the large categories or systems of understanding that we use in our negotiations with reality, specifically, in the case of narrative, with the problem of temporality: man's time-boundedness, his consciousness of existence within the limits of mortality." For a detailed examination of the history and nature of narrative, see Robert Scholes and Robert Kellogg, *The Nature of Narrative* (New York: Oxford University Press, 1968).

11. Cf. Scholes and Kellogg: "By narrative we mean all those literary works which are distinguished by two characteristics: the presence of a story and a story-teller. A drama is a story without a story-teller" (*Nature of Narrative,* p. 4). This general distinction is that between telling and showing, which received its classical formulation in the separation of diegesis from mimesis (Plato). Narrators, however, may be covert or overt, and this can sometimes obscure the above distinction. Seymour Chatman, *Story and Discourse: Narrative Structure in Fiction and Film* (Ithaca, N.Y.: Cornell University Press, 1983), pp. 33–34), expands narrative to include the covert and dramatic: "[Narrator] should mean only the someone—person or presence—actually telling the story to an audience, no matter how minimally evoked his voice or the audience's listening ear. A narrative that does not give the sense of this presence, one that has gone to noticeable lengths to efface it, may reasonably be called 'nonnarrated' or 'unnarrated.' (The seeming paradox is only terminological. It is merely short for 'a narrative that is not explicitly told' or 'that avoids the appearance of being told.') Thus there is no reason for positing some third category of narrative (like 'dramatic' or 'objective' or the like) since that is essentially 'nonnarrated' narrative."

12. In literature this threefold relation of author, narrator, character is immediately problematized because of the separation of the real author and narrator. In texts we cannot identify the narrator either with the real author or with what is called the implied author. The latter is derived from considering the text in all its attributes and not simply from those pertaining to the narrator. See Chatman, *Story and Discourse,* chap. 4.

13. David Carr offers convincing arguments for this position in *Time, Narrative, and History* (Bloomington: Indiana University Press, 1986). Beginning, as we have, from a Husserlian basis, he maintains that the beginning-middle-end structure is common to most of our experiences, even at the level of basic and nonverbal actions. The work is a polemic against those (especially philosophers of history) who maintain that narrative structure is imported from art to life and that life initially does not share this structure.

14. MacIntyre, *After Virtue,* p. 214.

15. Robert Champigny, *The Ontology of Narrative: An Analysis* (The Hague: Mouton, 1972), p. 29, makes important conceptual distinctions between acts and events: "Acts belong to experience; events are conceived. Events are reflections of acts in a temporal field." Acts, for Champigny, are ontologically primary in that they are the experiential underpinning for both conception and personhood. If I am right, they serve a similar role to that of Kantian intuitions, which without concepts are blind. On the question of the subject, Champigny claims that "acts are not activities of someone or something. They are 'substantial'; they are not attributes or accidents of substances. Acts, qualities, are felt. The question 'Felt by whom?' would be inappropriate on this level" (p. 31). We temporalize experience and its significance in conceiving it, and in doing so we also and necessarily personify ourselves and locate ourselves as historical subjects. There is much in Champigny's work that fits amiably with our present enterprise.

16. Paul Ricoeur, "On Interpretation," in *Philosophy in France Today,* ed. A. Montefiore (Cambridge: Cambridge University Press, 1983), p. 178.

17. Ibid., p. 178.

18. Paul Ricoeur, "History as Narrative and Practice" (*Philosophy Today,* Fall 1985), p. 214.

19. Ibid., p. 213.

20. L. Mink, "History and Fiction as Modes of Comprehension" (*New Literary History,* vol. 1, 1969–70), p. 557.

21. MacIntyre, *After Virtue,* p. 212.

22. Barbara Hardy, "Towards a Poetics of Fiction: 3. An Approach through Narrative" (*Novel,* vol. 2, no. 1, Fall 1968), p. 5.

23. Ricoeur, "On Interpretation," p. 181.

24. Ricoeur, *Time and Narrative,* vol. 3, p. 74.

25. Ibid., vol. 1, p. 3.

26. Carr, *Time, Narrative, and History,* p. 99.

27. Ricoeur, *Time and Narrative,* vol. 1, p. 74.

28. See ibid., p. 75.

29. For a useful guide to the work, see David Pellauer, "*Time and Narrative* and Theological Reflection" (*Philosophy Today,* Fall 1987).

30. Cf. Hans-Georg Gadamer: "Understanding is always an interpretation, and hence interpretation is the explicit form of understanding." *Truth and Method* (New York: Seabury Press, 1975), p. 274.

31. Ricoeur, *Time and Narrative,* vol. 1, p. 41.

32. Paul Ricoeur, *Hermeneutics and the Human Sciences: Essays on Language, Action and Interpretation* (New York: Cambridge University Press), p. 294.

33. C. Taylor, "Self-Interpreting Animals," *Human Agency and Language.* Further references to this work will be entered in the text as SA.

34. R. G. Collingwood, *The Principles of Art* (New York: Oxford University Press, 1978), adopts a similar view with respect to emotions and language: "the expression of emotion is not, as it were, a dress made to fit an emotion already existing, but is an activity without which the experience of that emotion cannot exist. Take away the language, and you take away what it expressed; there is nothing left but crude feeling at the merely psychic level" (p. 244). Collingwood's account is particularly useful for understanding the nature of unexpressed emotions and the effect on them of linguistic (and other) expression.

35. Cf. Gadamer: "Being that can be understood is language." *Truth and Method,* p. 432. This enigmatic statement is not intended to equate being with language, it simply claims that our understanding invariably occurs in language (construed broadly).

36. It is this *trace* that is retraced in memorial intentionality, refigured in remembering. Remembering is thus a reenactment.

37. See Ricoeur, *Time and Narrative,* vol. 1, p. 75.

38. C. Taylor, "The Significance of Significance: The Case of Cognitive Psychology," in *The Need for Interpretation: Contemporary Conceptions of the Philosopher's Task,* ed. S. Mitchell and M. Rosen (London: Humanities Press, 1983), p. 146.

39. Ricoeur, *Time and Narrative,* vol. 1, p. 75.

40. Ibid. This need for atonement is especially important in Ricoeur's work.

41. G. Santayana, *Scepticism and Animal Faith* (New York: Dover, 1955), pp. 158f, 252, and 257.

42. Arendt, *Human Condition,* p. 193.

43. Max Scheler, *Formalism in Ethics and Non-Formal Ethics of Values,* trans. M. Frings and R. Funk (Evanston, Ill.: Northwestern University Press, 1973), p. 385.

44. See Paul Ricoeur, "The Function of Fiction in Shaping Reality" (*Man and World,* vol. 12, no. 2, 1979, pp. 123–41.

45. Taylor, *Human Agency and Language,* p. 34.

46. Ibid., p. 103.

47. See ibid., chap. 1, "What is Human Agency?" Further references to this work will be added to the text as *Agency.*

48. MacIntyre, *After Virtue,* p. 221.

49. C. Taylor, *Sources of the Self: The Making of the Modern Identity* (Cambridge,

Mass.: Harvard University Press, 1989).

50. Ibid., p. 27.

51. Ibid., p. 47.

52. Cf. ibid., p. 514.

53. Stanley Hauerwas and David Burrell, "From System to Story: An Alternative Pattern for Rationality in Ethics," in Stanley Hauerwas, *Truthfulness and Tragedy: Further Investigations in Christian Ethics* (Notre Dame, Ind.: University of Notre Dame Press, 1977). Page references will be added to the text preceded by the initials HB.

54. In *Time and Narrative,* Ricoeur stresses the value of narrative as an ethical force. Fictional literature provides the reader with examples of imaginative variations on ways of living a life and these are rarely, if ever, ethically neutral: "reading becomes a provocation to be and to act differently" (3:249).

55. See Jean-François Lyotard, *The Postmodern Condition: A Report on Knowledge,* trans. G. Bennington and B. Massumi (Minneapolis: University of Minnesota Press, 1984).

56. See MacIntyre, *After Virtue,* p. 222.

57. See H. White, in W. J. T. Mitchell, ed., *On Narrative* (Chicago: University of Chicago Press, 1984), p. 14.

58. On this theme, see Julia Kristeva, *Powers of Horror: An Essay on Abjection,* trans. Leon Roudiez (New York: Columbia University Press, 1982), pp. 140ff.

59. This is Hegel's problem at the beginning of the *Phenomenology of Spirit.*

60. E. Benveniste, *Problems in General Linguistics* (Coral Gables, Fla.: University of Miami Press, 1971), p. 227.

61. See, for example, Michel Foucault, "What Is an Author?" *Language, Counter-Memory, Practice: Selected Essays and Interviews,* ed. Donald Bouchard (Ithaca, N.Y.: Cornell University Press, 1981). All of Foucault's work operates within the paradigm of what has been called the "death of the author."

3. The Subject

1. Cf. Benveniste on Aristotle's categories: "Now it seems to us—and we shall try to show—that these distinctions are primarily categories of language and that, in fact, Aristotle, reasoning in the absolute, is simply identifying certain fundamental categories of the language in which he thought." *Problems in General Linguistics* (PGL), p. 57.

2. An interesting case in point is autism. The autistic child, for example, has no grasp of language and none of the understanding that goes with it. The behavior associated with this lack is a certain self-absorption that cuts most social ties. As one writer has said, "The capacity for language, for talking, accompanies a capacity to care about whether anyone talks to you; autistic children don't care." Vicki Hearn, *Adam's Task: Calling Animals by Name* (New York: Knopf, 1986), p. 251. Such children seem to live in a world where reliance on others occurs only for their material and bodily needs. Much of the time autistic children are quite happily absorbed in sensory phenomena. Lack of language leaves these children at what might be called an animal level, a level that lacks the social and cultural dimensions of the language user. Whereas we may attempt to integrate them into our world, there is little or no reciprocity on the part of autistic children. Even to think of an autistic person as having a world similar to the language user's is begging the question. Language not only operates on the perceptually given, imbuing it with a meaning it would otherwise lack, but also goes a long way toward constituting what we mean by being a self, a person. As Hearn writes, " 'Why learn language?' is identical to the question 'Why be human (what we mean by human) at all?' In most cases, our humanity is in

place before we can ask the question, because most of us learn language so quickly and easily that we are already in and of the problem; autism is not a problem." (p. 252) The example of autistic children is a good illustration of what Benveniste is expressing in his distinction between the sensory-motor and the representative functions.

3. Cf. Husserl: "Everything has its name, or is nameable in the broadest sense, i.e., linguistically expressible." In Jacques Derrida, *Edmund Husserl's Origin of Geometry: An Introduction,* trans. John Leavey (New York: Nicolas Hayes, 1978), p. 162.

4. Benveniste also adds the following important line: "We can never get back to man separated from language and we shall never see him inventing it" (PGL, p. 224).

5. See Benveniste, PGL, chap. 21.

6. See Calvin Schrag, *Communicative Practice and the Space of Subjectivity* (Bloomington: Indiana University Press, 1986), p. 124.

7. See ibid., pp. 122ff., for a useful interpretation of this quotation from Benveniste.

8. Helen Keller, *The World I Live In* (New York: Century, 1908), pp. 113, 117, and 160.

9. F. de Saussure, *Course in General Linguistics,* trans. Wade Baskin (New York: Philosophical Library, 1959), pp. 111–12. The contention that language prefigures thought and that questions of real-world reference are to be omitted from a structuralist account of meaning has been discounted by various commentators. Saussure's statement that "language is a system of independent terms in which the value of each term results solely from the simultaneous presence of the others" (p. 114) is treated by Michael Devitt and Kim Sterelny as both "surprising" and "objectionable." *Language and Reality: An Introduction to the Philosophy of Language* (Cambridge, Mass.: MIT Press, 1987), p. 213). For example, in the structuralist claim that "brown" functions and is meaningful only in relation to other color words, Devitt and Sterelny see only a problematic rejection of reference, for "part of the meaning of 'brown' is given by the fact that it refers to brown things" (p. 213). But clearly this circular statement has problems of its own, and only momentarily puts off the question concerning those real-world entities that we call "brown" things. See their chap. 13 for a discussion of these issues.

10. In the case of animals, structure is generated through the exigencies of their lives; they must behave in certain fixed and ordered patterns if they are to survive. In Keller's case, one can imagine that such thoroughgoing purposes were lacking in her life.

11. One important implication of our account of the subject is that personhood is dependent on expression, and more particularly on the predication of the implied subject of utterances to the site of their production (the body). The person is, as I have said, an embodied subject. This position implies that preverbal children and certain individuals with serious language disorders, such as Helen Keller, are not, strictly speaking, persons. I think this is correct, especially if we consider the social responsibility that accrues to persons. However, this does not mean such individuals are therefore to be treated like animals and perhaps disposed of as one might dispose of an animal. Children are on their way to becoming persons, and this future must be respected. In the case of Keller, and many others like her, the possibility for self-conscious expression should not be ruled out, even if this requires the learning of special sign languages. At the other extreme, persons who have lost their means of expression (through brain damage, seizure, etc.) may indeed no longer have any self-awareness and little possibility of regaining it. In the latter case a certain retrospective respect for the person is understandable; it recognizes the possibility of a reprieve of the disability.

12. There are some interesting parallels here to the famous Turing test of artificial intelligence. See A. M. Turing, "Computing Machinery and Intelligence," in D. Hofstadter and D. Dennett, *The Mind's I* (New York: Bantam, 1982).

13. J. Lacan, *Ecrits: A Selection* (New York: Norton, 1977), pp. 86–87.

14. War provides an interesting example of negation and alienation in their ethical dimensions. As a morally responsible person one cannot kill another subject, another person. The "enemy" must be objectified, must not be allowed to speak; they must be regarded under a category of thingness, or at least as "them." Only he who is immoral can annihilate without guilt what is clearly constituted as another person, as "you." This latter situation provides a definition of evil. Alienation is already on the way to this condition. It is interesting to note in this respect that the category of the "third person" does not function like "I" and "you," for it passes outside the discourse to an "objective" reference. As Benveniste observes, "Certain languages show that the 'third person' is indeed literally a 'non-person'" ("The Nature of Pronouns," in *Problems of General Linguistics*).

15. Our usual application of the person concept is in fact fairly flexible, including babies, malformed individuals, people with artificial limbs, and such like.

16. This process usually occurs with animals only if we first personify their gestures, that is, see them as expressive of a certain subjectivity and as analogous to our speech.

17. James, *Principles of Psychology*, pp. 288, 323.

18. See Husserl, Investigation 1 in *Logical Investigations*, vol. 1, trans. J. N. Findlay (New York: Humanities Press, 1970). The *Bedeutung-Sinn* dichotomy is more pronounced in Husserl's *Ideas: General Introduction to Pure Phenomenology* (New York: Collier Books, 1975); see section 124. *Bedeutung* is there reserved for linguistic or ideal meaning.

19. Husserl, *Logical Investigations*, p. 269.

20. It is important to note that in the *Logical Investigations* Husserl separates the "content," or meaning, from the "object" referred to; see pp. 290f.

21. See ibid., p. 327.

22. This break of meaning from its authorial intention, original audience, and original context are themes common to hermeneutics, and may be found throughout the writings of both Gadamer and Ricoeur.

23. J. Derrida, *Margins of Philosophy*, trans. Alan Bass (Chicago: University of Chicago Press, 1982), p. 317.

24. J. Derrida, *Speech and Phenomena*, trans. David Allison (Evanston, Ill.: Northwestern University Press, 1973), p. 115.

25. Derrida's important essay "Signature, Event, Context" aims at these conclusions primarily by considering the indeterminate nature of context, the situation out of which utterances are to be interpreted. This is not to deny meaning itself, for linguistic or written signs must by definition be meaningful; it is to deny that an "intended meaning" cannot be univocally encoded in language. This is the basis of Derrida's notion of "dissemination," which he maintains is different from the more hermeneutic assumption of polysemia. The latter, according to Derrida, still has traces of an origin that a traditional hermeneutic investigation aims to disclose or recover, while dissemination avoids such an origin. This is, however, more a critique of traditional nineteenth-century than of contemporary hermeneutics.

26. Husserl, *Ideas*, §124. See also Husserl, "The Origin of Geometry": "Thus men as men, fellow men, world . . . and, on the other hand, language, are inseparably intertwined. . . ." In Derrida, *Edmund Husserl's Origin of Geometry*, p. 162.

27. Derrida, *Speech and Phenomena*, p. 85, footnote. Constitution is at the very heart of Husserl's phenomenology, going hand in hand with the notion of intentionality.

28. Husserl, *Logical Investigations,* pp. 279–80.
29. See Derrida, *Speech and Phenomena,* p. 58.
30. See Husserl, *Logical Investigations,* p. 275.
31. See Husserl, *Ideas,* §124.
32. This is very much like the way some of us read to ourselves. Because one thinks one must know already, one does not actually attempt to express oneself fully to oneself; it is deemed superfluous. Language in fact tolerates quite a degree of misuse; one need not say everything and one need not state it in correct grammatical form for a certain point to get across. This is a way of reformulating Husserl's position.
33. See Derrida, *Margins of Philosophy,* p. 318.
34. Although I think there are numerous important philosophical implications to this separation of ideality from meaning, it would take us too far from our primary topic to pursue them here.
35. This translation paradigm is one way of interpreting Gadamer's notion of the "fusion of horizons," which always involves this important claim: "one understands differently if one understands at all" (*Truth and Method,* p. 264).
36. Merleau-Ponty, *Phenomenology of Perception,* p. 401.
37. A. Lingis, "The Signs of Consciousness" (*Substance,* vol. 13, no. 1, 1984). Here Lingis is following Derrida, *Speech and Phenomena,* p. 76.
38. Derrida, *Speech and Phenomena,* p. 79.
39. Cf. Derrida: "Speech and the consciousness of speech—that is to say consciousness simply as self-presence—are the phenomenon of an auto-affection lived as the suppression of 'differance.' That *phenomenon,* that lived reduction of the opacity of the signifier, are the origin of what is called presence." *Of Grammatology,* trans. Gayatri Spivak (Baltimore: Johns Hopkins University Press, 1982), p. 166. Presence is thus the overlooking or suppression of the mediating signifier, or, which is the same thing, the erasing of a primordial difference or otherness. (Magritte's paintings often point to this overlooking: *Ceci n'est pas une pipe,* for example.) This self-presence is thus fundamentally alienated, in much the same way as a child's identity is gained in and through an other (e.g., the mother) or as Narcissus discovers himself in a reflection.
40. If expression indeed creates being, then this desire is also the desire to be and to be known. Sartre was close to this position when he described consciousness as nothingness, as a form of vacancy that must act in order to be.
41. One might wish to add to the Cartesian cogito the fact that I not merely am but am also "here" and "now," thus giving an initial affirmation of being spatiotemporally located. The further explanation of such relative locations, as Hegel stressed in the beginning of the *Phenomenology,* would still have to be determined. The answer we have been pursuing lies in narrative emplotment. Already in the Heideggerian notion of being-in-the-world we find an overcoming of the Cartesian dualism and a recognition of the inextricable situatedness of the subject.
42. There are also physical-biological answers, which are not of direct interest here on account of their reductive nature.
43. M. Merleau-Ponty, "The Child's Relations with Others," trans. William Cobb, in *The Primacy of Perception,* ed. James Edie (Evanston, Ill.: Northwestern University Press, 1971), p. 151.
44. For the account that follows, see Lacan, "The Mirror Stage as Formative of the Function of the I," *Ecrits.*
45. The "real" is not what we tend to mean by "reality," for this is primarily a symbolic product. As an aside, Lacan does allow the female subject a closer relationship to the real than the male, with a respective loss of the symbolic. See Kaja Silverman, *The Subject of Semiotics* (New York: Oxford University Press, 1983), p.

186.

46. Lacan, "The Function and Field of Speech and Language in Psychoanalysis," *Ecrits,* p. 68. This position of Lacan's was derived primarily from Lévi-Strauss's ideas on the prepersonal nature of symbolic social structures.

47. This distinction is evidenced in the way Proust, for example, (re)captures himself in the textual identity of the character Marcel.

48. I am here summarizing Lacan's exposition in *Ecrits,* pp. 1–6. Also see Merleau-Ponty, "The Child's Relations with Others," p. 125.

49. The syncretic stage is also continued, both in the experience of one's bodily unity and in certain forms of sympathetic identification with others.

50. The influence of Hegel on Lacan's dialectic of self and other should be clear here.

51. Merleau-Ponty, "The Child's Relations with Others," pp. 118–19; this was written eleven years after Lacan's address, to which Merleau-Ponty refers.

52. A point we have especially learned from the later work of Heidegger.

53. Schutz, *Phenomenology of the Social World;* see esp. chap. 2. A chronicle, such as the *Annals of Saint Gall* (see Hayden White, "The Value of Narrativity," in *On Narrative,* ed. W. J. T. Mitchell (Chicago: University of Chicago Press, 1981), p. 7, tends to list a calendar of events that exhibit little in the way of emplotment, reports of the weather being placed on equal footing with the death of a king. The chronicle, while selective, leaves one wondering about the historical import of the events recorded.

54. The hermeneutic epistemological stance that I have outlined does not, of course, preclude our rejecting interpretations because of a straightforward misrepresentation of the "facts." Interpretation that aims at truth must begin from an adequate grasp of the spatial and temporal details of the course of events to be understood, much as textual interpretation must account for and begin from what is actually given in the text—which will include certain words and phrases with sedimented and accepted meanings.

55. Julia Kristeva, "The Speaking Subject," in *On Signs,* ed. Marshall Blonsky (Baltimore: Johns Hopkins University Press, 1985), p. 217. Cf. Heidegger on anxiety in "What is Metaphysics": "Anxiety robs us of speech. Because beings as a whole slip away, so that just the nothing crowds round, in the face of anxiety all utterance of the 'is' falls silent." *Basic Writings,* ed. David Krell (New York: Harper and Row, 1977), p. 103. In other words, anxiety, for Heidegger, severs the threads of intentionality that allow us a lived-through familiarity and complacency with the world; in so doing it opens the possibility for resignification. However, Heidegger's interests are more ontological (concerning Dasein's authenticity) than explicitly psychological.

56. Language used against tradition is a major theme in Julia Kristeva, *Revolution in Poetic Language,* trans. Margaret Waller (New York: Columbia University Press, 1984).

57. On the relation between displacement-condensation and metonymy-metaphor, see R. Coward and J. Ellis, *Language and Materialism: Developments in Semiology and the Theory of the Subject* (Boston: Routledge and Kegan Paul, 1980), chap. 6.

58. This epistemologically creative dimension of poetic discourse was pursued to great effect by Gaston Bachelard in his postscientific works. See esp. his *Poetics of Space.*

59. See, for example, Freud's "The Relation of the Poet to Day-Dreaming" of 1908 and Christopher Caudwell, *Illusion and Reality: A Study of the Sources of Poetry* (New York: International Publishers, 1977). Art, however, may have a spirit of playfulness that is lacking in its psychological counterpart.

60. Lacan, "Sign, Symbol, Imaginary," in *On Signs,* p. 209. The repressed in this case is nothing other than an example of what we have called the prenarrative level.

61. J. Lacan, *The Four Fundamental Concepts of Psycho-Analysis,* trans. Alan Sheridan (New York: Norton, 1981), p. 20.

62. See Freud, *Introductory Lectures on Psychoanalysis* (Penguin Books, 1974), lecture 11.

63. Lacan, *Ecrits,* p. 88. The hermeneutical dimension of Lacan's approach is brought out well in the following statement by Peter Dews, *Logics of Disintegration: Post-Structuralist Thought and the Claims of Critical Theory* (New York: Verso, 1987), p. 66: "the effectivity of the past, like that of any present event in the subject's life, is determined by the manner of its interpretation: it is the way in which we understand our past, for Lacan, which determines how it determines us."

64. A process similar to that described here was seen in an earlier chapter to occur in relation to unexpressed emotions. Repression is the censoring of such emotions from conscious conceptual recognition or interpretation.

65. Lacan, *Ecrits,* p. 169.

66. R. Schafer, *Language and Insight* (New Haven, Conn.: Yale University Press, 1978), p. 6. Cf. Lacan, *Ecrits* p. 52: "What we teach the subject to recognize as his unconscious is his history—that is to say, we help him to perfect the present historization of the facts that have already determined a certain number of the historical 'turning points' in his existence." See also Paul Ricoeur, "The Question of Proof in Freud's Psychoanalytical Writings," *Hermeneutics and the Human Sciences,* p. 273: "Psychoanalytical reports are kinds of biographies and autobiographies whose literary history is a part of the long tradition emerging from the epic tradition of the Greeks, the Celts and the Germans."

67. Schafer, *Language and Insight,* p. 31.

68. Ibid.

69. Oliver Sacks, *The Man Who Mistook His Wife for a Hat and Other Clinical Tales* (New York: Harper and Row, 1987), pp. 110–11. The parallel with Schafer's position becomes evident from the following: "We have, each of us a life-story, an inner narrative—whose continuity, whose sense, *is* our lives. It might be said that each of us constructs and lives, a 'narrative,' and that this narrative *is* us, our identities. . . . Each of us *is* a singular narrative, which is constructed, continually, unconsciously, by, through, and in us—through our perceptions, our feelings, our thoughts, our actions; and, not least, our discourse, our spoken narrations. . . . To be ourselves we must *have* ourselves—possess, if need be repossess, our life-stories."

70. Cf. Ricoeur, "The Question of Proof," p. 253: "But what is it to remember? It is not just to recall certain isolated events, but to become capable of forming meaningful sequences and ordered connections. In short, it is to be able to constitute one's own existence in the form of a story where a memory as such is only a fragment of the story."

71. I shall not consider in any detail the precise models and mechanisms of mind that Freud offered in explanation of the processes that we are considering in this section. Such models and their terminology have a somewhat inconsistent history in Freud's thought. The processes at our present level of discussion are not only well documented in fields other than psychoanalysis (especially other forms of psychological therapy and literature), but are also applicable to much of our everyday lives.

72. See Donald Spence, *Narrative Truth and Historical Truth: Meaning and Interpretation in Psychoanalysis* (New York: Norton, 1984), chap. 6. The case history is not itself one or more of these stories, but rather plots the development of certain of them during the analytic sessions.

73. Spence, *Narrative Truth,* p. 288.

74. Ibid., p. 175.

75. Ibid., p. 31.

76. C. G. Jung, *Memories, Dreams, Reflections,* trans. Richard and Clara Winston (New York: Vintage Books, 1973), p. 3.

77. L. von Ranke, ed., *Sämtliche Werke* (Leipzig, 1867–90), bd. 33, viff.

78. Paul Veyne, *Writing History: Essay on Epistemology,* trans. M. Moore-Rinvolucri (Middletown, Conn.: Wesleyan University Press, 1984), pp. 71–72.

79. As B. Croce said, "Where there is no narrative, there is no history." (Quoted in Hayden White, "The Question of Narrative in Contemporary Historical Theory," *History and Theory,* no. 1, 1984, p. 3.) Frederick Olafson, in his thorough treatment of historical narrative in *The Dialectic of Action: A Philosophical Interpretation of History and the Humanities* (Chicago: University of Chicago Press, 1979), argues fairly convincingly that the proper object of historical investigation, human action, is invariably understood within a teleological setting (the teleology being internal to the history and defined in terms of the ends set by the agents involved) and that a narrative description is the most adequate in this domain. See esp. chaps. 3 and 4.

80. White, "The Question of Narrative," p. 2. As White says in *Tropics of Discourse* (Baltimore: Johns Hopkins University Press, 1985), p. 92, "Historians may not like to think of their works as translations of fact into fictions; but this is one of the effects of their works."

81. Quoted in White, "The Question of Narrative," p. 3, n. 4.

82. White, *Tropics of Discourse,* p. 94. White's final claim is interesting, for it points to what I have called the prenarrative level. If narrative style is "immanent in" the language in which we describe events (prior to explicit historical analysis and emplotment), and if we view language not simply as a tool but as disclosive of the world, then the world of human actions will invariably appear in a narrative structure.

83. As Arthur Danto states the matter in *Narration and Knowledge* (New York: Columbia University Press, 1985), p. xv, "since we plainly have no access to the world apart from our ways of thinking and talking about it, we scarcely, even in restricting ourselves to thought and talk, can avoid saying things about the world."

84. R. Barthes, "The Discourse of History," *Rustle of Language,* p. 127.

85. R. Barthes, *Image, Music, Text,* trans. Stephen Heath (New York: Hill and Wang, 1977), pp. 123–24. See Hayden White's account of this passage in "The Question of Narrative," p. 14.

86. Barthes, "The Discourse of History," p. 16.

87. Veyne, *Writing History,* p. x.

88. Cf. Veyne: "Then what are the facts worthy of rousing the interest of the historian? All depends on the plot chosen; in itself, a fact is not interesting or uninteresting . . . the fact is nothing without its plot." *Writing History,* p. 33.

89. "With this chapter we reach the goal that has never ceased to guide the progress of our investigation, namely, the actual refiguration of time, now become human time through the interweaving of history and fiction" (Ricoeur, *Time and Narrative* 3:180). Also: "the interweaving of history and fiction in the refiguration of time rests, in the final analysis, upon this reciprocal overlapping, the quasi-historical moment of fiction changing places with the quasi-fictive moment of history" (3:192).

90. Paul Veyne does make the claim that whereas literature, which is fictional, must generate interest by developing exciting or aesthetically pleasing plots and characters, history need simply relate the "truth," for in that an event actually happened (even though it may be boring) it carries an intrinsic interest value for the general reader. See *Writing History,* p. 11. It must be admitted that there is some

truth in this view, but it will not stand without certain provisos. One could, as a historical exercise, seek to discover what Emerson generally had for lunch on weekends and the precise manner of its preparation, or describe in detail what route he took on his morning walks. These would be historical "facts," but they would hardly hold the average reader's interest for long. Facts, as Veyne does go on to say, are nothing without the plot within which they take on significance. Irrelevant details have therefore little interest even though they may be correct. A second point to be noted is that literature is not exactly devoid of mimetic character. Though fiction might deal with imaginary characters and plots, there is still a mimetic relation operating that insists these fictional worlds be possible worlds, and as we know, the possible always stands in a dialectic with the actual. Fiction is perhaps more "factual" than Veyne is prepared to admit.

91. Both Gadamer and Habermas, for example, have rejected this claim of disinterestedness to be a profitable (and even possible) means of acquiring understanding and knowledge.

92. White, *Tropics of Discourse,* p. 99.

93. Further references to this work (Descartes, *Discourse on Method and Meditations,* trans. L. J. Lafleur [New York: Liberal Arts Press, 1960]), will be added to the text.

94. Cf. Husserl: "Between the meanings of consciousness and reality yawns a veritable abyss" (*Ideas,* §49).

95. See Immanuel Kant, *Critique of Pure Reason,* trans. Norman Kemp Smith (New York: St. Martin's Press, 1965), p. 246.

96. Husserl's phenomenology, while owing much to Descartes's method, in fact sought to remain between, and therefore outside, the two metaphysical options of *res cogitans* and *res extensa* by stressing "intentionality," though not always with success. Phenomenologically speaking, perception, for example, is in essence nothing but a presentation to a subject, and there is no thing in itself except as a derived theoretical construct.

97. Merleau-Ponty, *Phenomenology of Perception,* p. 400. Cf. Dalia Judovitz: "Reading philosophy no longer suffices to become a philosopher: rather, one has to become an epistemologist first, for the guarantee of certain knowledge takes precedence over historical knowledge itself. Moreover, this conception of philosophy in purely epistemological terms excludes from the domain of history that which belongs to its own history as a system of thought; it precludes the history of its own thought in order to found the evidence of its truth." "Autobiographical Discourse and Critical Praxis in Descartes" (*Philosophy and Literature,* vol. 5, 1981), p. 100. Montaigne, for example, works in the other direction, a reflection on history disclosing general and often contradictory characteristics of an always situated subject. More recently, the work of Michel Foucault stresses the way the self is generated through various technologies that serve to circumscribe and valorize the self and its functions. It is not that we come to know the self through our theorizing; rather we produce it through the practice of theory.

98. Merleau-Ponty, *Phenomenology of Perception,* p. 402.

99. Merleau-Ponty posits the existence of what he calls a "tacit cogito" preceding the spoken one, but his formulation seems to undermine itself when he admits that "The tacit *cogito* is a *cogito* only when it has found expression for itself" (*Phenomenology of Perception,* p. 404). This tacit cogito would appear to be parallel to what I have called subjectivity (one's sense of possible expression), which is perhaps synonymous with our sense of existence.

100. Cf. Jean Piaget, *Genetic Epistemology,* trans. Eleanor Duckworth (New York: Norton, 1971), pp. 45–46: "Language is certainly not the exclusive means of

representation [of action]. It is only one aspect of the very general function that Head has called the symbolic function. I prefer to use the linguists' term: the semiotic function. . . . In addition to language the semiotic function includes gestures, either idiosyncratic or, as is the case of the deaf and dumb language, systematized. It includes deferred imitation. . . . It includes drawing, painting, modelling. It includes mental imagery. . . . Language is but one among these many aspects of the semiotic function, even though it is in most instances the most important."

101. In *The Raw and the Cooked,* trans. J. and D. Weightman (London: Cape, 1970), Lévi-Strauss took the structures of the social world back, in Kantian fashion, to an architecture of the mind. This form of reduction leads to a transcendentalism which supports the synchronic or atemporal analyses that Lévi-Strauss preferred, but this view is perhaps at odds with many of his essential insights into the symbolic and its functioning in differential relations.

102. It no longer seems correct to say that "man" speaks, as though language were a mere instrument at the mercy of our wills, but it seems similarly incorrect to say simply that "language" speaks (a move instigated by Mallarmé and Heidegger), unless we can somehow feed human subjects back into "language." Both approaches have something important to say about our embeddedness in language. It can be seen that I have been supporting a middle view: I indeed speak, but I *am* only insofar as I *do.* The various works of Michel Foucault illustrate this point. His general method is to trace the workings of power (or "technologies") that serve to define man via the exclusions they inaugurate. This exclusion occurs through various dominant discourses about the state, sexuality, madness, etc. The result of Foucault's work is not the eradication of the subject (as is sometimes supposed) but an historical or genealogical investigation into the ways we come to define and hence delimit ourselves in our discourse and practices. See Foucault's Vermont lecture, "Technologies of the Self," in *Technologies of the Self: A Seminar With Michel Foucault,* ed. L. H. Martin, H. Gutman, and P. H. Hutton (Amherst: University of Massachusetts Press, 1988).

103. Barthes, "The Death of the Author," *Image, Music, Text,* pp. 145, 147. Further references to this work will be added to the text preceded by IMT.

104. Which is not to say that emotions (and affectivity generally) have no cognitive value, for they are intimately linked to our understanding. Moods, as Heidegger has shown, cast a certain meaning over the world, disclose it in new ways.

105. R. Barthes, *Roland Barthes,* trans. Richard Howard (New York: Hill and Wang, 1984).

106. M. Foucault, *Language, Counter-Memory, Practice: Selected Essays and Interviews,* trans. Donald Bouchard and Sherry Simon (Ithaca, N.Y.: Cornell University Press, 1981), p. 137.

107. Ibid., p. 138.

108. Barthes, *Roland Barthes,* p. 143. Barthes also offers an interesting quotation from Diderot: "Everything has happened in us because we are ourselves, always ourselves, and never one minute the same" (p. 144). This important theme of identity in difference is one I have already discussed.

109. Ibid., p. 60.

110. I am especially indebted to Kaja Silverman, *Subject of Semiotics,* for this model. See her chap. 5.

111. Certain computer mailings could be exempted from the normal category of authorship.

112. See Ricoeur, *Time and Narrative,* vol. 1, chap. 3.

113. See Ricoeur's use of the term *relinquishment* in part 2 of *Hermeneutics and the Human Sciences.*

114. Cf. Wolfgang Iser, "The Reading Process," in *Reader-Response Criticism: From Formalism to Post-Structuralism,* ed. Jane Tompkins (Baltimore: Johns Hopkins University Press, 1981), p. 67: "In thinking the thoughts of another, his [the reader's] own individuality temporarily recedes into the background, since it is supplanted by these alien thoughts. . . . As we read, there occurs an artificial division of our personality, because we take as a theme for ourselves something that we are not."

115. Part of the ploy of much contemporary literature (especially what is called self-conscious fiction or metafiction) is to bring to the fore this manipulatory moment by frustrating the reader's normal identifications. This break can be made, for example, by explicitly parading the text's textual and written nature, much as a film shot may pan back to reveal the film crew and equipment.

116. Cf. Martin Heidegger, *Being and Time,* trans. John Macquarrie and Edward Robinson (New York: Harper and Row, 1962). I am using "state of mind" in a less technical sense than Heidegger's *Befindlichkeit,* and more in line with the standard meaning of the phrase in English.

117. These characteristics of the embodied subject have both temporary and more permanent aspects. That is, many of our states are fairly ephemeral, while others serve as one's underlying and relatively abiding habitus.

118. Subjectivity (the possibility of expression) is also allied to proprioception (the sensory awareness of our body that serves as a basis for action) on the purely bodily level.

119. See Roman Jakobson, "Shifters, Verbal Categories, and the Russian Verb," *Word and Language* (The Hague: Mouton, 1971).

120. Roy Schafer draws a similar conclusion from a psychoanalytic viewpoint: "Personal development may be characterized as change in the questions it is urgent or essential to answer. As a project in personal development, personal analysis changes the leading questions that one addresses to the tale of one's life and the lives of important others" (in *On Narrative,* ed. W. J. T. Mitchell, p. 31).

121. Taylor, *Human Agency and Language, Philosophical Papers I,* p. 75.

Conclusion

1. Bruce Wilshire, *Role Playing and Identity: The Limits of Theatre as Metaphor* (Bloomington: Indiana University Press, 1982), p. 227, states that "One *is* one's 'roles' but not *just* one's 'roles,' for one is also an unobjectifiable consciousness of 'roles' actual and possible—even roles as yet unimagined." In contrast to my exposition, Wilshire emphasizes the importance of prethematic role playing (based in mimetic social behaviour on the part of a body-self) for his view of self and does not, in my mind, place enough emphasis on the linguistic and narrative aspects prefiguring and refiguring our consciousness of such roles.

2. Being *as,* which is fundamental to a hermeneutic ontology, also has interesting mimetic connotations. We view ourselves not only as someone but also as *like* someone. For example, we view our life story as being tragic, perhaps like Hamlet's or Othello's. We use such models (or archetypes) more or less consciously when we tell our own story.

3. Roman Ingarden, *The Literary Work of Art,* trans. George Grabowicz (Evanston, Ill.: Northwestern University Press, 1973); see chap. 10.

4. The "ethical" argument of existentialists such as Sartre that all role identifications of the human subject are forms of "inauthenticity," forms of denying one's freedom, seems on our account to fly in the face of fact. At most one can say that certain representations of an individual are insufficient with respect to that individual's diversity, possibilities, and history.

5. Merleau-Ponty, *Phenomenology of Perception,* p. 402. Merleau-Ponty con-

tinues: "the speaking subject plunges into speech without imagining the words he is about to utter. . . . The word 'sleet,' when it is known to me, is not an object which I recognize through any identificatory synthesis, but a certain use made of my phonatory equipment, a certain modulation of my body as a being-in-the-world" (p. 403).

6. I do not imply by the word *dematerialize* any metaphysical option for what is called in philosophy "materialism."

7. A useful critique of the mind-body problem can be found in G. B. Madison, "The Hermeneutics of (Inter)subjectivity, or: The Mind/Body Problem Deconstructed," *Man and World,* vol. 21, 1988, pp. 3–33.

8. In this respect, sleep without dreams is surely a temporary extinguishing of the self.

9. This shift can be easily mapped onto my earlier distinction of the experiencing versus the narrating self. My position parallels that of G. H. Mead in *Mind, Self, and Society from the Standpoint of a Social Behaviorist,* ed. Charles Morris (Chicago: University of Chicago Press, 1962), p. 142: "I know of no other form of behavior than the linguistic in which the individual is an object to himself, and, as far as I can see, the individual is not a self in the reflective sense unless he is an object to himself."

10. Merleau-Ponty, *Phenomenology of Perception,* p. 392.

11. Michel Foucault, *Madness and Civilization: A History of Insanity in the Age of Reason* (New York: Vintage Books, 1973).

BIBLIOGRAPHY

Arendt, Hannah. *The Human Condition.* Chicago: University of Chicago Press, 1981.

Bachelard, Gaston. *The Poetics of Space,* trans. M. Jolas. Boston: Beacon Press, 1968.

Barthes, Roland. *Image, Music, Text,* trans. Stephen Heath. New York: Hill and Wang, 1977.

———. *Roland Barthes,* trans. Richard Howard. New York: Hill and Wang, 1984.

———. *The Rustle of Language,* trans. Richard Howard. New York: Hill and Wang, 1986.

Beckett, Samuel. *Three Novels by Samuel Beckett: Malloy, Malone Dies, The Unnamable.* New York: Grove Press, 1965.

Benamou, M., and C. Caramello, eds. *Performance in Postmodern Culture.* Madison, Wis.: Coda Press, 1977.

Benveniste, Emile. *Problems in General Linguistics,* trans. Mary Meek. Coral Gables, Fla.: University of Miami Press, 1971.

Blonsky, Marshall, ed. *On Signs.* Baltimore: Johns Hopkins University Press, 1985.

Booth, Wayne. *The Rhetoric of Fiction.* Chicago: University of Chicago Press, 1961.

Bourdieu, Pierre. *Outline of a Theory of Practice,* trans. Richard Nice. New York: Cambridge University Press, 1982.

Brooks, Peter. *Reading for the Plot: Design and Intention in Narrative.* New York: Vintage Books, 1985.

Bruner, Jerome. *Actual Minds, Possible Worlds.* Cambridge, Mass.: Harvard University Press, 1986.

Bultmann, Rudolf. *New Testament and Mythology and Other Basic Writings,* trans. Schubert M. Ogden. Philadelphia: Fortress Press, 1984.

Carr, David. *Time, Narrative, and History.* Bloomington: Indiana University Press, 1986.

Casey, Edward S. *Remembering: A Phenomenological Study.* Bloomington: Indiana University Press, 1987.

Caudwell, Christopher. *Illusion and Reality: A Study of the Sources of Poetry.* New York: International Publishers, 1977.

Champigny, Robert. *The Ontology of Narrative: An Analysis.* The Hague: Mouton, 1972.

Chatman, Seymour. *Story and Discourse: Narrative Structure in Fiction and Film.* Ithaca, N.Y.: Cornell University Press, 1983.

Collingwood, R. G. *The Principles of Art.* New York: Oxford University Press, 1978.

Coward, R., and J. Ellis. *Language and Materialism: Developments in Semiology and the Theory of the Subject.* Boston: Routledge and Kegan Paul, 1980.

Crites, Stephen. "The Narrative Quality of Experience." *Journal of the American Academy of Religion,* vol. 39, no. 3, September 1971.

Danto, Arthur. *Narration and Knowledge.* New York: Columbia University Press, 1985.

Dennett, Daniel. *Brainstorms: Philosophical Essays on Mind and Psychology.* Cambridge, Mass.: MIT Press, 1981.

Derrida, Jacques. *Edmund Husserl's Origin of Geometry: An Introduction,* trans. John P. Leavey. New York: Nicolas Hayes, 1978.

———. *Margins of Philosophy,* trans. Alan Bass. Chicago: University of Chicago Press, 1982.

———. *Of Grammatology,* trans. Gayatri Spivak. Baltimore: Johns Hopkins Press, 1982.

———. *Speech and Phenomena,* trans. David Allison. Evanston, Ill.: Northwestern University Press, 1973.

Descartes, René. *Discourse on Method and Meditations,* trans. L. J. Lafleur. New York: Liberal Arts Press, 1960.

Descombes, Vincent. *Objects of All Sorts: A Philosophical Grammar,* trans. L. Scott-Fox and J. Harding. Baltimore: Johns Hopkins University Press, 1986.

Dewart, Leslie. *Evolution and Consciousness: The Role of Speech in the Origin and Development of Human Nature.* Toronto: University of Toronto Press, 1989.

Dews, Peter. *Logics of Disintegration: Post-Structuralist Thought and the Claims of Critical Theory.* New York: Verso, 1987.

Dilthey, Wilhelm. *Pattern and Meaning in History: Thoughts on History and Society,* ed. H. P. Rickman. New York: Harper and Row, 1962.

Dray, William, ed. *Philosophical Analysis and History.* New York: Harper and Row, 1966.

Foucault, Michel. *Language, Counter-Memory, Practice: Selected Essays and Interviews,* ed. Donald Bouchard. Trans. Donald Bouchard and Sherry Simon. Ithaca, N.Y.: Cornell University Press, 1981.

———. *The Order of Things: An Archeology of the Human Sciences,* translation of *Les mots et les choses.* New York: Vintage Books, 1973.

Freud, Sigmund. *Introductory Lectures on Psychoanalysis,* trans. James Strachey. Penguin Books, 1974.

Gadamer, Hans-Georg. *Truth and Method,* translation of *Wahrheit und Methode.* New York: Seabury Press, 1975.

Gallie, W. B. *Philosophy and the Historical Understanding.* New York: Schocken Books, 1964.

Hardy, Barbara. "Towards a Poetics of Fiction: 3. An Approach through Narrative." *Novel,* vol. 2, no. 1, Fall 1968.

Hauerwas, Stanley, and David Burrell. "From System to Story: An Alternative Pattern for Rationality in Ethics." In Stanley Hauerwas, *Truthfulness and Tragedy: Further Investigations in Christian Ethics.* Notre Dame, Ind.: University of Notre Dame Press, 1977.

Hearn, Vicki. *Adam's Task: Calling Animals by Name.* New York: Knopf, 1986.

Heidegger, Martin. *Basic Writings,* ed. David Krell. New York: Harper and Row, 1977.

———. *Being and Time,* trans. John Macquarrie and Edward Robinson. New York: Harper and Row, 1962.

Hofstadter, D., and D. Dennett. *The Mind's I: Fantasies and Reflections on Self and Soul.* New York: Bantam Books, 1982.

Hume, David. *A Treatise of Human Nature.* Oxford: Clarendon Press, 1981.

Husserl, Edmund. *Cartesian Meditations: An Introduction to Phenomenology,* trans. Dorian Cairns. The Hague: Martinus Nijhoff, 1970.

———. *Ideas: General Introduction to Pure Phenomenology,* trans. W. R. Boyce Gibson. New York: Collier Books, 1975.

———. *Logical Investigations,* vol. 1, trans. J. N. Findlay. New York: Humanities Press, 1970.

Ingarden, Roman. *The Literary Work of Art,* trans. George Grabowicz. Evanston, Ill.: Northwestern University Press, 1973.

Jakobson, Roman. *Word and Language.* The Hague: Mouton, 1971.

James, William. *The Principles of Psychology.* Cambridge, Mass.: Harvard University Press, 1983.

Judovitz, Dalia. "Autobiographical Discourse and Critical Praxis in Descartes." *Philosophy and Literature,* vol. 5, 1981.

Jung, C. J. *Memories, Dreams, Reflections,* trans. Richard and Clara Winston. New York: Vintage Books, 1973.

Kant, Immanuel. *Critique of Pure Reason,* trans. Norman Kemp Smith. New York: St. Martin's Press, 1965.

Keller, Helen. *The World I Live In.* New York: Century, 1908.

Kemp, Peter, and David Rasmussen. *The Narrative Path: The Later Works of Paul Ricoeur.* Cambridge, Mass.: MIT Press, 1989.

Koselleck, Reinhart. *Futures Past: On the Semantics of Historical Time,* trans. Keith Trieb. Cambridge, Mass.: MIT Press, 1985.

Kristeva, Julia. *Revolution in Poetic Language,* trans. Margaret Waller. New York: Columbia University Press, 1984.

Lacan, Jacques. *Ecrits: A Selection,* trans. Alan Sheridan. New York: Norton, 1977.

———. *The Four Fundamental Concepts of Psycho-Analysis,* trans. Alan Sheridan. New York: Norton, 1981.

Lingis, Alphonso. "The Signs of Consciousness." *Substance,* vol. 13, no. 1, 1984.

Locke, John. *An Essay Concerning Human Understanding.* New York: Dover, 1959.

Lyotard, Jean-François. *The Postmodern Condition: A Report on Knowledge,* trans. G. Bennington and B. Massumi. Minneapolis: University of Minnesota Press, 1984.

MacIntyre, Alisdair. *After Virtue: A Study in Moral Theory.* Notre Dame, Ind.: University of Notre Dame Press, 1984.

Madison, G. B. "The Hermeneutics of (Inter)subjectivity, or: The Mind/Body Problem Deconstructed." *Man and World,* vol. 21, 1988, pp. 3–33.

Mead, George H. *Mind, Self, and Society from the Standpoint of a Social Behaviorist,* ed. Charles Morris. Chicago: Chicago University Press, 1962.

Merleau-Ponty, Maurice. *Phenomenology of Perception,* trans. Colin Smith. London: Humanities Press, 1978.

———. *The Primacy of Perception,* ed. James Edie. Evanston, Ill.: Northwestern University Press, 1971.

Mink, Louis. "History and Fiction as Modes of Comprehension." *New Literary History,* vol. 1, 1969–70.

Mitchell, S., and M. Rosen, eds. *The Need for Interpretation: Contemporary Conceptions of the Philosopher's Task.* London: Humanities Press, 1983.

Mitchell, W. J. T., ed. *On Narrative.* Chicago: University of Chicago Press, 1981.

Montefiore, A., ed. *Philosophy in France Today.* Cambridge: Cambridge University Press, 1983.

Nietzsche, Friedrich. *The Will to Power,* trans. Walter Kaufmann and R. J. Hollingdale. New York: Vintage Books, 1968.

Olafson, Frederick A. *The Dialectic of Action: A Philosophical Interpretation of History and the Humanities.* Chicago: University of Chicago Press, 1979.

Olney, James. *Metaphors of Self: The Meaning of Autobiography.* Princeton, N.J.: Princeton University Press, 1981.

Parfit, Derek. *Reasons and Persons.* Oxford: Clarendon Press, 1984.

Pellauer, David. "*Time and Narrative* and Theological Reflection." *Philosophy Today,* Fall 1987.

Piaget, Jean. *Genetic Epistemology,* trans. Eleanor Duckworth. New York: Norton, 1971.

Polkinghorne, Donald. *Narrative Knowing and the Human Sciences.* Albany, N.Y.: SUNY Press, 1988.

Proust, Marcel. *On Art and Literature, 1896–1919,* trans. Sylvia Townsend Warner. New York: Carroll and Graf, 1984.

———. *Remembrance of Things Past,* 2 vols., trans. Scott Moncrieff. New York: Random House, 1934.

Ricoeur, Paul. *The Conflict of Interpretations,* ed. Don Ihde. Evanston, Ill.: Northwestern University Press, 1974.

———. *Hermeneutics and the Human Sciences: Essays on Language, Action and Interpretation,* trans. John B. Thompson. New York: Cambridge University Press, 1983.

———. "The Function of Fiction in Shaping Reality." *Man and World,* vol. 12, no. 2, 1979, pp. 123–41.

———. "History as Narrative and Practice," trans. Robert Lechner. *Philosophy Today,* Fall 1985.

———. *Time and Narrative,* 3 vols., trans. Kathleen McLaughlin and David Pellauer. Chicago: University of Chicago Press, 1984–88.

Sacks, Oliver. *The Man Who Mistook His Wife for a Hat and Other Clinical Tales.* New York: Harper and Row, 1987.

Santayana, George. *Scepticism and Animal Faith.* New York: Dover, 1955.

Sarbin, Theodore. *Narrative Psychology: The Storied Nature of Human Conduct.* New York: Praeger, 1986.

Saussure, F. de. *Course in General Linguistics,* trans. Wade Baskin. New York: Philosophical Library, 1959.

Schafer, Roy. *Language and Insight.* New Haven, Conn.: Yale University Press, 1978.

Schaffer, Elinor, ed. *Rhetoric and History: Comparative Criticism Yearbook.* Cambridge: Cambridge University Press, 1981.

Scheler, Max. *Formalism in Ethics and Non-Formal Ethics of Values,* trans. M. Frings and R. Funk. Evanston, Ill.: Northwestern University Press, 1973.

Scholes, Robert, and Robert Kellogg. *The Nature of Narrative.* New York: Oxford University Press, 1968.

Schrag, Calvin. *Communicative Practice and the Space of Subjectivity.* Bloomington: Indiana University Press, 1986.

Schutz, Alfred. *The Phenomenology of the Social World,* trans. G. Walsh and F. Lehnert. Evanston, Ill.: Northwestern University Press, 1967.

Silverman, Kaja. *The Subject of Semiotics.* New York: Oxford University Press, 1983.

Spence, Donald. *Narrative Truth and Historical Truth: Meaning and Interpretation in Psychoanalysis.* New York: Norton, 1984.

Taylor, Charles. *Human Agency and Language: Philosophical Papers I.* Cambridge: Cambridge University Press, 1985.

———. *Sources of the Self: The Making of the Modern Identity.* Cambridge, Mass.: Harvard University Press, 1989.

Tompkins, Jane P., ed. *Reader-Response Criticism: From Formalism to Post-Structuralism.* Baltimore: Johns Hopkins University Press, 1981.

Unamuno, Miguel de. *Tragic Sense of Life,* trans. J. E. Crawford Flitch. New York: Dover, 1954.

Veyne, Paul. *Writing History: Essay on Epistemology,* trans. Mina Moore-Rinvolucri. Middletown, Conn.: Wesleyan University Press, 1984.

White, Hayden. "The Question of Narrative in Contemporary Historical Theory." *History and Theory,* no. 1, 1984.

———. *Tropics of Discourse: Essays in Cultural Criticism.* Baltimore: Johns Hopkins University Press, 1985.

Wilshire, Bruce. *Role Playing and Identity: The Limits of Theatre as Metaphor.* Bloomington: Indiana University Press, 1982.

INDEX

ANTHONY PAUL KERBY is Assistant Professor of Philosophy at the University of Ottawa. He has published a number of articles on narrative and hermeneutics, and is a founding member of the Canadian Society for Hermeneutics and Postmodern Thought.

www.ingramcontent.com/pod-product-compliance
Lightning Source LLC
LaVergne TN
LVHW040157080826
844660LV00001B/4

* 9 7 8 0 2 5 3 3 3 1 4 3 4 *